Getting It
All Done

HBR WORKING PARENTS SERIES

*Tips, stories, and strategies for
the job that never ends.*

The **HBR Working Parents Series** supports readers as they anticipate challenges, learn how to advocate for themselves more effectively, juggle their impossible schedules, and find fulfillment at home and at work.

From classic issues such as work-life balance and making time for yourself to thorny challenges such as managing an urgent family crisis and the impact of parenting on your career, this series features the practical tips, strategies, and research you need to be—and feel—more effective at home and at work. Whether you're up with a newborn or touring universities with your teen, we've got what you need to make working parenthood work for you.

Books in the series include:

Advice for Working Dads

Advice for Working Moms

*Communicate Better with
   Everyone*

Getting It All Done

Managing Your Career

Taking Care of Yourself

WORKING PARENTS

Tips, stories, and strategies for the job that never ends.

Getting It All Done

Harvard Business
Review Press
Boston, Massachusetts

The web addresses referenced in this book were live and correct at the time of the book's publication but may be subject to change.

Library of Congress Cataloging-in-Publication Data

Names: Harvard Business Review Press.
Title: Getting it all done / Harvard Business Review.
Other titles: HBR working parents series.
Description: Boston, Massachusetts : Harvard Business Review Press,
    [2020] | Series: HBR working parents series | Includes index.
Identifiers: LCCN 2020026435 (print) | LCCN 2020026436 (ebook) |
    ISBN 9781633699755 (paperback) | ISBN 9781633699762 (ebook)
Subjects: LCSH: Work and family. | Parenting. | Work-life balance.
Classification: LCC HD4904.25 .G5346 2020 (print) | LCC HD4904.25
    (ebook) | DDC 646.7—dc23
LC record available at https://lccn.loc.gov/2020026435
LC ebook record available at https://lccn.loc.gov/2020026436

ISBN: 978-1-63369-975-5
eISBN: 978-1-63369-976-2

The paper used in this publication meets the requirements of the American National Standard for Permanence of Paper for Publications and Documents in Libraries and Archives Z39.48-1992.

CONTENTS

Introduction

Getting to "All Done" xiii

Grab the tricks and tools that will help you
and start using them today.

by Daisy Dowling, Series Editor

Section 1

Strategy for Supper

Bring Your Work Skills Home

1. To Have a Happier Home Life, 3
Treat It a Little More Like Work

Plan and schedule, play to everyone's
strengths, and put people first.

by Whitney Johnson

2. The Agile Family Meeting 9

Transform your family by asking three
questions.

by Bruce Feiler

3. Sync Up Your Family Calendars 17

With fewer bad surprises, everyone is happier.

by Elizabeth Grace Saunders

Contents

4. Negotiating with Your Kids   25

Reach better outcomes and model
a better process.

by Mary C. Kern and Terri R. Kurtzberg

5. Assemble Your "Parenting Posse"   35

Networking helps at home, too.

by Alison Beard

Section 2

Say No to Doing Everything

Put Your Real Priorities First

6. Does Your Schedule Reflect Your Values?   47

Learn to translate your priorities into action.

by Elizabeth Grace Saunders

7. Let Go of the Idea of Balance   55

Look for four-way wins.

An *HBR IdeaCast* Interview with
Stewart D. Friedman and Alyssa F. Westring

8. How to Spend Your Parenting Time and Energy Wisely   65

When was the last time you checked in
on your kids' priorities?

by Amy Jen Su

9. **"Delegating with Joy"**   75

   To get the help you need, put a task and an ask in a higher context.

   A *Women at Work* Interview with Tiffany Dufu

10. **Too Much to Do? Here's How to Ask for Help**   83

    Figure out what you need, just ask for it, and accept what is offered.

    by Heidi Grant

11. **How to Say No to Taking on More**   89

    Practice saying it out loud.

    by Rebecca Knight

Section 3

Getting It All (Mostly) Done
Productivity Tips and Hacks You Need

12. **Working from Home When You Have Kids**   99

    It takes more than a home office.

    by Daisy Dowling

13. **You Can Make Family Meals Happen**   107

    Consider family breakfast.

    by Daisy Dowling

14. **Getting Things Done While Locked Down with Your Kids**   115

    Advice for the pandemic—and beyond.

    Contributed by 18 HBR readers

15. **How Working Parents Can Manage the Demands of School-Age Kids**   127

    Strategies to handle the chaos.

    by Daisy Dowling

16. **Stop Feeling Guilty About Your To-Do List**   135

    Make peace with never being caught up.

    by Rebecca Knight

Section 4

You Can't Be in Two Places at Once

Deal with Tough Work-Family Conflicts

17. **Winning Support for Flexible Work**   145

    Propose a plan that works for you, your boss, and your company.

    by Amy Gallo

18. How to Handle Work When Your Child Is Sick   151

What to say to your boss and colleagues.

by Daisy Dowling

19. What to Do When Personal and Professional Commitments Compete for Your Time   159

Strategies for when you can't be in two places at once.

by Elizabeth Grace Saunders

20. Keep Your Home Life Sane When Work Gets Crazy   165

Make sure to communicate with the people who matter most.

by Stewart D. Friedman

21. Managing Work During a Family Crisis   171

Four tactics to juggle your job, your kids, and your own well-being.

by Sabina Nawaz

Contents

Epilogue

You've Got This

22. ### Parenting Is Making You a Better Leader   183

    Help them grow.

    by Peter Bregman

Notes   191

About the Contributors   193

Index   199

INTRODUCTION

Getting to "All Done"

by Daisy Dowling

A few years ago, when my daughter was a toddler, she would finish her breakfast with a triumphant ritual. After spooning up the last of her cereal, she'd shout "All done!" and beam with delight, then slam her fist down on the plastic tray table of her high chair with a loud *bang* for emphasis. Every morning, without fail, it was the same thing: the same sense of joyous competence at being able to handle the task in front of her, that same sense of completion and closure. I loved to watch her, but as embarrassing as this is to admit, I felt a little jealous. As a full-time working parent, I wasn't in a "competence and completion" state of mind. In fact, it was more the reverse. By the time each morning's Great Oatmeal Take-Down had concluded, around 6:45 a.m., I was already well underwater and trying desperately to swim up to the surface. Emails had rolled in overnight from colleagues waiting for answers. I had to hustle if I was going to make it to that 8 a.m. meeting. There was the leaky sink I needed to have fixed and tax forms to sign and get to the post office, and my boss was waiting on the draft strategy report, and oh, the laundry pile (which could only be described as Himalayan) and mounting eldercare "issues" to handle, and was I getting to get to the gym *once* this week? "Getting it all done?" Who are we kidding? I was behind all day and every day—and it felt crummy.

Are you a working parent trapped in that same always-on-but-never-finished scramble? Maybe you've tried to cope with your endless to-do list by working later into the night, or breaking it up into multiple lists, or using a new calendar color-coding system or special task-tracking app to help you get more accomplished. Even so, are you still struggling to find the bandwidth for things you know are important—like networking, or *really* preparing for that big meeting next week, or reading to the kids, or sitting down for a family dinner? Day to day, despite stretching yourself to your personal limits, do you still harbor a hazy but nagging sense that you should *be getting more done* at work and *be there more* for your children? Have you ever considered wholesale life changes—like quitting your job or moving to a remote area, off the grid—just to get some relief and to feel on top of things, "together," and like yourself again?

The vast majority of parents I coach would answer "yes" to one or more of these questions, and if you did also, I actually take that as a fundamentally healthy and positive sign. If work and career obligations are this top-of-mind for you, that's a strong, objective indicator that you're a diligent and conscientious professional. If *being there* for the kids looms large in your daily thoughts, it's proof-positive you're a devoted parent. Your intentions are good, and your heart is 100% in the right place. And it's precisely *because* they are that it's so jarring when you can't deliver on everything you're supposed to.

Sure, there's the practical problem of actually cranking through your to-do's at work and at home. In normal circumstances, that's already a major challenge—and in the past year or more, throughout the Covid-19 pandemic, it's never been more acute. (How can you do your full-time job, run the household, be a parent, and teach your kids the whole third-grade curriculum at the same time? C'mon—you'd have to be able to bend the laws of time and space to get *that* all done.) Yet the bigger, more insidious problem here—the one that my clients find even more painful—isn't the practical one. It's the *feeling* of always being behind, of falling short, of being at odds with their own values and aspirations. *If I'm such a hard worker, why can't I finish everything I need to? If I'm such an attentive parent, why can't I figure out how to cook and eat dinner with the kids each night?* That "All done!" feeling seems *very* far away—if possible to reach at all.

Enter this book: your realistic, 3D road map for getting a whole lot closer. I'll tell you up front: This collection of articles doesn't attempt to be the end-all guide to personal productivity, and it won't engage in any philosophical debate or politics about the feasibility of "having it all." What it will do for you is something quite different, yet very powerful: Whatever the circumstances of your career or family life, it will meet you where you live, today. It will offer you new skills and tricks for shortening and taming your to-do list and for feeling more in control as you do so. It will teach you how to bring your work skills home and your home skills to work, how to prioritize more thoughtfully and effectively, how to get more done in the time you *do* have available, and how to diffuse the conflict that can rear up when you're pulled in two (or more) directions at once. It will show you how to attack the "getting it all done" problem from all sides and, no matter how long your to-do list remains, build your own sense of competence and completion. The ideas in this book worked for me, they've worked for my clients—and they'll work for you, as a working parent also.

I recommend that you read these pieces with an eye on your own needs, trusting your own intuition. Maybe Bruce Feiler's ideas on effective family meetings will help you tame the weekly chaos, or Rebecca Knight's advice on saying "no" will help you have less of "it all" to get done in the first place, or Alison Beard's look at why and how to build your "parenting posse" will help you get the support you need when things get extra busy. Just as this book does, think broadly and work the problem from all different angles. There's a terrific buffet of ideas here. Grab the tricks and tools that will help you and start using them.

And then, at the end of those days when you've tried your level best to do well at work and be a loving parent, give yourself permission to close the laptop, put your to-do list aside—and, putting your hand down firmly on the table for emphasis, tell yourself, *All done*.

Section 1

Strategy
for Supper

Bring Your Work Skills Home

To Have a Happier Home Life, Treat It a Little More Like Work

by Whitney Johnson

Quick Takes

- Schedule your day to allow for surprises
- Gather all your family members' views before making big decisions
- Play to everyone's strengths
- Treat everyone as a VIP

N ot long ago, I spent almost three weeks on the road, doing meetings and talks in multiple countries and a couple of U.S. cities, too. I enjoyed the travel and the work, but it was with relief that I returned home. I was ready to relax.

But I didn't find the refuge I'd hoped for. I was confronted by not only all the business matters I'd neglected while away but also the myriad tasks and errands I needed to do for my family, friends, and church congregation. Eager as I was to reengage with all of them, home didn't feel restful. It felt busy, demanding, and a little chaotic.

I articulated my frustration in a weekly newsletter and was surprised by the response. Many people seem to find, as I do, that their life at work runs more smoothly than their life at home does.

For a house and family to operate smoothly, we need to employ many of the same tactics we use at the office: planning and scheduling, thoughtful decision making, and putting people first.

- **Schedule your day to allow for surprises.** When I'm on the job, I keep to a detailed schedule. Everything is accounted for, and time is incorporated to allow for unexpected surprises. I'm now trying to run my home life in the same way, so I can get everything done efficiently and effectively and have time left over to create meaningful experiences with my family and rejuvenate myself. I haven't yet mastered it (I have an assistant who helps me stay organized at work!), but that doesn't mean I can't try.

- **Gather input.** When I need to make a big decision at work, I consult with my team. The final call might be mine, but I want to hear everyone's considered opinions first. At home, it's historically been so much easier to just decide, sometimes consulting with my family, sometimes not. This is changing, though. We're currently in the process of moving, and, rather than managing by fiat, something that would never happen at the office, we are consciously taking all views into account. Our kids are 18 and 22, which helps. But, as I've discovered at work, the most junior people (or children) often provide valuable, even crucial, input.

- **Identify and develop strengths.** In my professional life, I also think carefully about developing the people on my team—about where they are on their learning curve, how they add value, and what they can do to apply and hone their skills. We recently administered the Clifton Strengths

Finder throughout the organization to identify strengths so that we can play to them. Of course, most parents are constantly working to help their children grow into successful adults. But we can be even more deliberate about it. Over the holidays, each member of our family also took the strengths test. We then read the results aloud and discussed how we might help one another better leverage those assets.

- **Treat everyone as important.** Perhaps the most important thing I do as a boss and business owner is try to treat every person with whom I work as the most important person in the world. I want to apply this ideal at home as well. At work, I wouldn't dream of not turning toward the person I'm talking to and giving them my full attention, whether client or coworker. And yet, too many times to count, I idly check my phone while my husband or children are speaking. With a little prodding from our high-school-senior daughter, I've started to focus more on face time (and not the Apple variety). When we spend more time chatting like this, it leaves me not depleted but invigorated—feeling better connected to the people who matter most to me.

When you're a parent with a full-time job, much of the work of home is compressed into a few hours a day, the same hours in which you'd like to relax. But we can't feel entitled to the latter. Entitlement, which I have called the sneaky saboteur of our career aspirations, doesn't serve us well at home, either. It takes planning and effort to make a household and family run smoothly. If I want to chill out, I have to earn it.

Adapted from content posted on hbr.org, February 21, 2019 (product #H04T70).

The Agile Family Meeting

by Bruce Feiler

Quick Takes

Start with one meeting per week with just three questions:

- What worked well in our family this week?
- What didn't work well in our family this week?
- What will we agree to work on this week?

amilies around the world are searching desperately for fresh techniques for managing their household chaos. One proven solution that my family, along with many others, uses comes from an unlikely source: agile development.

It's no secret that working parents face enormous pressures. Ellen Galinsky, of the Families and Work Institute, asked a thousand children, "If you were granted one wish about your parents, what would it be?" When she asked parents to predict what their children would ask for, the parents said: "spending more time with us." They were wrong. The kids' number-one wish: that their parents were less tired and less stressed.

So how can we reduce that stress and help families to become happier?

I spent the last 15 years trying to answer that question, meeting families, scholars, and experts ranging from the founder of the Harvard Negotiation Project to online game designers to Warren Buffett's bankers. I published my findings in the bestselling book *The Secrets of Happy Families*. The single best solution I found may be the simplest of all: Hold regular family meetings to discuss how you're managing your family.

Meet the First Agile Family

A few years ago, my research brought me to the Starr family home in Hidden Springs, Idaho. The Starrs are an ordinary American family with their share of ordinary American family issues. David is a software developer; Eleanor is a stay-at-home mom. Their four children range in age from 10 to 15.

Like many parents, the Starrs were trapped in that endless tension between the sunny, smooth-running household they aspired to be living in and the exhausting, ear-splitting one they were actually living in. "I tried the whole 'love them and everything will work out' philosophy," Eleanor said, "but it wasn't working. 'For the love God,' I said, 'I can't take this anymore.'"

What the Starrs did next, though, was surprising. Instead of turning to their parents, their peers, or even a professional, they looked to David's workplace. Specifically, to a philosophy of business problem solving that David has studied and taught: agile development. The techniques worked so well for their family that David wrote a white paper about it, and the idea spread from there.

When my wife, Linda, and I adopted this blueprint in our weekly family meetings, it quickly became the single most impactful idea we had introduced into our home since the birth of our children.

The Three Questions

The idea of agile was invented in the 1980s in large measure through the leadership of Jeff Sutherland. A former fighter pilot in Vietnam, Sutherland was chief technologist at a financial firm in New England when he began noticing how dysfunctional software development was. Companies followed the "waterfall model," in which executives issued ambitious orders from above that then flowed down to harried programmers below. "Eighty-three percent of projects came in late, over budget, or failed entirely," Sutherland told me.

Sutherland created a new system, in which ideas flowed not just down from the top but up from the bottom, in which groups were designed to react to changes in real time. The centerpiece is a weekly meeting that's built around shared decision making, open communication, and constant adaptability.

Such meetings are easy to replicate in families. In my home, we started when our twin daughters were five and chose Sunday afternoons. Everyone gathers around the breakfast table; we open with a short, ritualistic drum tapping on the table; then, following the agile model, we ask three questions.

1. What worked well in our family this week?

2. What didn't work well in our family this week?

3. What will we agree to work on this week?

From the very beginning, the most amazing things started coming out of our daughters' mouths. What worked well in our family this week? "Getting over our fears of riding a bike." "We've been doing much better making our beds." What went wrong? "Doing our math sheets." "Greeting visitors at the door."

Like most parents, we had found our children to be something of a Bermuda Triangle: Words and thoughts would go in, but few ever came out. Their emotional lives had been invisible to us. The family meeting provided that rare window into their innermost thoughts.

The most satisfying moments came when we turned to the topic of what we would work on during the coming week. The girls loved this part of the process, particularly selecting their own rewards and punishments. Say hello to five people this week, and get an extra 10 minutes of reading before bed. Kick someone; lose dessert for a month. Turns out they were little Stalins.

Naturally, there was a gap between the girls' off-the-charts maturity during these 20-minute sessions and their behavior the rest of the week, but that didn't matter. It felt to us as if we were laying massive underground cables that wouldn't fully light up their world for many years to come. Ten years later, we are still holding these family meetings every Sunday. Linda counts them as among her most treasured moments as a mom.

So what did we learn?

1. Empower the children

Our instinct as parents is to issue orders to our children. We think we know best; it's easier; who has time to argue? And besides, we're usually right! There's a reason few systems have been more "waterfall" than the family. But as all parents quickly discover, telling your kids the same thing over and over is not necessarily the best tactic. The single biggest lesson we learned from our experience with agile practices is to reverse the waterfall as often as can be. Enlist the children whenever possible in their own upbringing.

Brain research backs up this conclusion. Scientists at the University of California and elsewhere found kids who plan their own time, set weekly goals, and evaluate their own work build up their prefrontal cortex and other parts of the brain that help them exert greater cognitive control over their lives. These so-called executive skills aid children with self-discipline, avoiding distraction, and weighing the pros and cons of their choices. By participating in their own rewards and punishment, children become more intrinsically motivated.

2. Parents aren't invincible

Another instinct we have as parents is to build ourselves up, to be Mr. or Ms. Fix-it. But abundant evidence suggests this type of leadership is no longer the best model. Researchers have found that the most effective business teams are not dominated by a charismatic leader. Instead, in these teams, members spend as much time talking to one another as to the leader. They meet face-to-face regularly, and everyone speaks in equal measure.

Sound familiar? "One thing that works in family meetings," David Starr told me, "is the kids are allowed to say whatever they want, even about the grown-ups. If I've come back from a trip and am having trouble reentering the routine, or if mom hasn't been nice that week, this is a safe venue in which to express their frustration."

3. Build in flexibility

Another assumption parents often make is that we have to create a few overarching rules and stick to them indefinitely. This philosophy presumes we can anticipate every problem that will arise over the years. We can't. A central tenet of the tech sector is if you're doing the same thing today you were doing six months ago, you're doing something wrong. Parents can learn a lot from that idea.

The agile family philosophy accepts and embraces the ever-changing nature of family life. It's certainly not lax;

think of all the public accountability. And it's not anything goes. But it anticipates that even the best designed system will need to be reengineered midstream.

• • •

As I was leaving the Starrs' home, I asked Eleanor what was the most important lesson I should learn from the first agile family.

"In the media, families just *are*," she said. "But that's misleading. You have your job; you work on that. You have your garden, your hobbies; you work on those. Your family requires just as much work. The most important thing agile taught me is that you have to make a commitment to always keep working to improve your family."

What's the secret to a happy family, in whatever situation you may find yourself and despite whatever kind of stress you face?

Try.

Adapted from content posted on hbr.org, June 26, 2020 (product #H05P9E).

Sync Up Your Family Calendars

by Elizabeth Grace Saunders

Quick Takes

- Decide on a central location

- Agree on how events are added

- Touch base daily

- Have a weekly huddle

No, I'm still working. I thought you were serving the kids dinner at 6?!

Mom, I have a school play tomorrow morning.

Why didn't I know that you would be out of town and the babysitter couldn't come this whole week until Sunday night???

Keeping track of your own commitments is challenging enough. But when you add on coordinating kids' schedules on top of what you already need to do for work and life, a solid family calendar system is essential to reduce stress and diminish avoidable bad surprises.

In my experience as a time management coach for many working parents, I've seen that there isn't one right way to keep track of your family's schedule. But there are some basic principles that can guide you in setting up a system that works effectively and helps you all to feel like you're on the same team.

Decide on a Central Location

As a family, you need to decide on a set place where you put commitments as they come up and where you check for those commitments on a daily basis. Many families use electronic calendar and task systems like Google Calendar or apps like Cozi, OurHome, or Any.do. With these tools, you can have a different color for each family member's calendar, share calendars, set up recurring events, and schedule reminders. But in addition to these tech options, you can also write down commitments on a whiteboard or large wall calendar posted in a central location. If you have young children, the visual on the wall can be effective as a way for them to see anything that specifically applies to them. And if you have kids (or a spouse) who tend to think of things as out of sight, out of mind, the bold visual reminder of what's happening for the week can be exceptionally helpful.

Agree on How Events Are Added

If all adults and kids in the household are old enough and on board with adding events to a shared calendar, that's the easiest solution for keeping the family schedule up to date. Have each adult in the home, as well as the children, be responsible for adding their own items when they become aware of them. And then have the adults in the house be responsible for adding events that apply to the whole family.

However, as a time management coach, I know that "ideal systems" doesn't always work so it's good to have some backup options. If one spouse or partner is willing and able to put things on the calendar and the other isn't, set up an agreement that every day any new scheduling information is passed on to the person who is willing to enter it. The same holds true for kids. If one or more children aren't old enough or strong enough on follow-through to consistently add commitments, ask them to immediately give papers or forward information to the adult who is willing to get them onto the schedule. That way, on a daily basis, the calendars should be up-to-date. Also, all adults, including nannies or babysitters, should have access to the kids' calendars to add or modify events as needed.

Have a Weekly Huddle

Each week, have a conversation with your spouse, partner, or co-parent on what's happening in the upcoming week that you both need to coordinate on the schedule. That could mean talking through drop-off and pickup for sports and activities, any special school event, prep that needs to be done ahead of a deadline, or any travel. If you have a babysitter or other childcare providers who need to be aware of the schedule, designate one of you to communicate with them about expectations.

This weekly conversation is the opportunity to work through any challenges before they become emergencies. Often, these meetings work best on Sunday afternoons, but you can adjust the timing to suit your needs. I recommend reserving at least 30 minutes to review the weekly schedule as a recurring event on your calendar. Even if this meeting can't happen at the exact same time each week, don't let it drop off your agenda. Talking through the next seven days will save you from having to reschedule meetings at the last minute to make it to a school event or frantically calling your kids' friends' parents to see if they can bring your child home after practice.

If you choose to do a paper wall calendar or whiteboard calendar, update it with the main events for the week right after the meeting. If you use both, this will help your virtual calendars and physical calendars to stay in sync.

Touch Base Daily

Every day, make sure you and your spouse or partner are touching base about the next day's schedule. A time that usually works well to do this is right after the kids go to bed so that you're talking things through before you're falling asleep yourself. But if your children are older and don't need your help with their bedtime routine, you can also do this after dinner. Confirm that both of you are on the same page about when you're going to and from work, who is doing kid drop-off and pickup, and any special events like sports or after-hours work commitments.

If your kids are older and have more complex schedules, make sure that you've also talked through the calendar with them before they go to sleep (or you go to sleep). Make sure you all know what they have going on tomorrow and if there is anything that will need your help. It's better to be aware the night before that they need you to drive them to school to bring in a large board for their school project instead of finding out during breakfast.

Go Beyond the Basics

Once you've mastered the essentials of making sure that fixed commitments are on the calendar, then you can add other activities that could help life run more smoothly. For example, you may designate a certain time for meal planning and grocery shopping each week or a time to do laundry so you're not always wondering how to squeeze those activities in. Or you may set aside certain times to exercise or spend quality time with your kids. Adding these types of activities to your calendar can help you to remember how you want to spend your time instead of simply letting the time slip away.

Even with a great calendar system, there still will be unexpected items that come up. Kids are experts at keeping life interesting. But by deciding on—and sticking to—a calendar system that works for you and your family, you can dramatically reduce stress around managing the day-to-day.

Negotiating with Your Kids

by Mary C. Kern and Terri R. Kurtzberg

Quick Takes

- Sidestep emotions and recognize repetitive arguments

- Prepare like you would for a negotiation at work

- Know what you're trying to accomplish

- Ask questions

- Present ideas in ways that appeal

You're going to negotiate with your kids today, probably multiple times. According to one informal survey of 2,000 parents, we negotiate with our children an average of six times a day (lasting about eight minutes each, or 24 hours a month).[1]

Unfortunately, parents often feel that these negotiations don't go well. In our experience as social scientists, professors, and with our own kids—as well as through discussions with hundreds of parents while researching our book *Negotiating at Home: Essential Steps for Reaching Agreement with Your Kids*—we heard story after story of parents who were highly effective at the conference table but less so around the dinner table. One successful executive explained that he routinely received compliments on his negotiation skills at work, but at home he often found himself resorting to "Go ask your mother!" when faced with an irrational, shortsighted third-grader. When reminded that he often negotiated with irrational, shortsighted business clients, he was perplexed.

Stumbling in Negotiations at Home

Why does this happen to people who can execute high-stakes deals, who can persuade their colleagues to take new points of view, and who can handle conversations about raises and promotions with ease? Three challenges of negotiating with our children stand out:

- **Emotion.** Our kids reach for different tools than our colleagues—guilt trips, meltdowns, playing one parent off the other—in no small part because they know they can't get fired, and neither can we! We also let ourselves act and react in more extreme ways than we would in the office. Successful negotiators at work know how to stay focused on the problem and not get sidetracked by interpersonal dynamics.

- **Repetition.** We engage in the same conversations—bedtime, screen time, mealtime—again and again, and thus fall into patterns and ruts in the ways we respond. At work, negotiations are more contained and don't tend to carry over as much from one situation to the next.

- **Preparation.** Because they're unannounced, because they're with our kids, and because they're often over everyday things like chores and dessert, we don't tend to plan for these negotiations or pre-pare psychologically. At work, we can often antici-pate a negotiation, and so do our due diligence and prepare ahead of time.

The problem isn't that professional negotiation skills don't apply at home—it's that we're not using them. In fact, bringing your professional expertise home can un-lock unrealized value in your negotiations with your kids. Working parents especially need to get to "win-win" agreements, which are those that protect the main interests of both sides. Time and energy are precious, and these agreements solve immediate problems, pre-vent their recurrence, strengthen your relationships, and enhance your family time. Here are some strategies to reach them.

Know What You're Really Here to Accomplish

At work, we are generally clear with ourselves about what we want out of a situation and see reaching our overarch-ing goal as a problem to be solved. At home, we get mired in specific positions and power struggles, which can dis-tract us from being open to more productive solutions. Think of the parent who successfully haggled with her child about wearing a hat outside. *When my daughter didn't want to wear her hat and had that look on her face that told me she was prepared to go to the mat over this, I instead proposed a game of Little Red Riding Hood. I told her my own scarf would be the hood and that I would get to be the star, upon which she begged to wear it.*

Instead of either just giving in or engaging in a winner-take-all battle of "hat or no hat," the parent realized that her central interest was keeping the child's head warm. Knowing what's most important, and what you can or cannot live without in an agreement, will help you stay true to your "north star" instead of getting stuck on any one idea.

Ask Questions to Fill in the Gaps

Nobody knows your kids better than you do. This is tremendously useful for negotiations, but since we can never fully know what's going on with another person in any given moment, this also creates a blind spot. *My child and I butted heads over a donut. He wanted the whole donut all at once, while I wanted to give him half first, and the second half if he still wanted it. It was ugly, and I finally gave in out of exasperation.*

If we had a disagreement like this at work, we would likely ask the colleague why they cared so much about it, but the parent skipped this step. When he offered the donut in two halves, he failed to account for the value his child placed on being able to bite into a giant, whole donut. Had he asked for his child's perspective, it might have changed the interaction in tone at least, if not in behavior. Offering the chance to participate and explain his side would also have helped inspire a sense of fair play.

Use the Right Approach at the Right Time

Every executive knows that some battles don't need to be fought at all, some might be strategically postponed, and others just need a firm decision made at the top. Parents similarly would benefit from choosing the right strategy for the right moment instead of engaging thoughtlessly. The same approach might land very differently as your kids grow up (or even based on whether they're hungry at that moment).

Decide when to disengage entirely (*I knew nothing good was going to come of continuing the conversation at that point, so I said we needed to table it until later*) and when to spend the time trying to better grasp the situation. And while "Because I said so!" is the right answer sometimes, if used too often our kids start to tune it (and you) out. Explaining how decisions get made can greatly increase compliance and goodwill.

Present Ideas in Ways That Appeal

Effective managers know that it's not just what you say, but how you say it. Busy parents can minimize contentious back-and-forth by crafting their statements to pave the way toward acceptance.

Go first. Much of your conversation will consist of offers and counteroffers, so use these to signal your own interests and your insight into their interests. State offers early in the negotiation to anchor the rest of the conversation by setting expectations and orienting subsequent counteroffers. *Offering a 10 p.m. curfew usually means my son asks for 11 in response, and we settle on 10:30. If he got to go first, he'd ask for midnight and then we'd end up settling at 11!*

Embed choice. Instead of a single offer, two or three choices, framed in terms of their priorities, make it easier for your kids to say yes. Choice gives a sense of control over both the process and outcome. A parent ordering takeout mastered this technique: *I announced where we would be ordering from instead of opening the floor for debate but allowed each child to choose a dish. This one small change sidestepped an ongoing moment of tension in our house.*

Highlight reference points. We consider offers not in isolation, but as compared to other alternatives. For example, an item on sale seems like a great deal in no small part because of the larger (original) price tag. This works because as compared to the "it could have been worse" option, the proposed option seems more palatable. *I told my teen that her actions could have resulted in a much more severe punishment, but that I would go easy on her and reduce it.*

Address fairness. "It's not fair!" is a common refrain, but kids' assumptions that fairness is based on everything being exactly equal can be overly simplistic and limiting. While splitting the cookie between siblings right down the middle is generally a good practice, perhaps the 4-year-old shouldn't get as much dessert as the teenager. Nor should the two kids split the last piece of cake in half if one prefers the icing and the other the cake. *In our house, we created a word—"unfaired"—to describe that feeling of injustice. When our kids use it, we can recognize that we understand why something might feel unfair to them, and then analyze why something might be fair even if it wasn't equal.*

Don't do all the talking. Silence can be a powerful tool. It can both help you avoid making unilateral concessions (like increasing your offers prematurely) and give your child a chance to contribute. *My son wanted to take the* *trolley back to the hotel after lunch, but I said I wanted to walk back to take advantage of the nice day. Instead of immediately overruling him, I paused. He then suggested that we walk in the opposite direction to get in a longer walk and take a longer trolley ride back.*

• • •

Successful managers know how to prioritize their goals, ask good questions, and put offers on the table in ways that inspire creativity and generate agreements that both sides want to say yes to. These same skills can help working parents (especially with today's increased at-home hours) create positive outcomes with their kids to both help navigate difficult moments and model effective problem-solving skills. Your kids continue to grow, and so must your skill set. And by practicing with your entrenched, passionate, persistent toddlers and teens, your kids may even make you better at your job.

Adapted from "How to Negotiate . . . with Your Kids," on hbr.org, May 29, 2020 (product #H05MY1).

Assemble Your "Parenting Posse"

by Alison Beard

Quick Takes

- Take time to engage with a wide variety of parents
- Offer to help drive a kid to practice or contribute to a class party
- Be generous with your encouragement—and what's worked for you
- Ask for help—even at the last minute
- Listen and learn from other parents

On a typical Monday, at the start of a super-busy workweek for me, one of my mom friends, Heather, got my daughter from school and kept her into the evening. On Tuesday, another mom friend, Nicolle, drove my son to his 5:45 p.m. basketball practice. On Wednesday, Tricia handled the cooking-class-to-home carpool. On Thursday, Sarah chaperoned both of our daughters at skating. And, on Friday, Rebecca helped me think through a tricky situation at the office.

I'm so grateful to have what every parent with a job outside the home needs: a parenting posse. This is a group of fellow moms and dads—at my kids' school, in our neighborhood, and at the office—who support me in the extremely messy business of balancing my work and my home lives.

You might not think that an upper-middle-class knowledge worker like me would need this help. My husband and I both have busy jobs but relatively flexible schedules. We're able to work from home. Right now, our business travel is limited. And we can afford to pay an afternoon sitter to assist with childcare and driving. But I suspect that we would struggle mightily to maintain our careers if we couldn't call on others to fill in the gaps.

In the past, grandparents, siblings, aunts, uncles, or cousins might have played this role. But most of us live and work too far away from our extended families for that to happen anymore. Friends must become family. When you're a working parent, especially one whose kids have grown out of simple daycare or nanny situations but can't yet drive or take public transportation on their own, that network—your posse—is how you survive.

Here's how to build and use one effectively.

Engage

When you're managing a demanding job and busy kids, there's a tendency to be laser-focused on whatever task is at hand. At the office, you bang away at your projects, attend all your meetings, and eat at your desk; you don't have time for coffee room chitchat or lunch with colleagues. At school or activity drop-offs and pickups, you aim to be in and out; at classroom or birthday parties, you focus on your kids, not the other parents. While understandable, these strategies are misguided; they might save you some time in the short term, but they prevent you from building the relationships key to long-term success in your work-life juggle.

Most of my cubemates at HBR—and many of the colleagues with whom I work closely—are also working parents. We talk a great deal about our kids: not just their ages and grades but also their academic highs and lows, extracurriculars, personality quirks, likes, and dislikes. We are closer colleagues because we share these stories—and more willing and able to help each other out. When I'm late for a podcast taping because I had to deliver a forgotten backpack, I can text my cohost Dan, who has three kids, and our producer, Curt, dad to a toddler, and they both understand. When I'm unexpectedly working from home because someone has come down with strep, my next-desk-over friend Amy, mom of two grown boys, emails me files with a sweet "I've been there" note.

In my personal life, I've learned to relish the moments I catch with other parents in the school lobby or on warm-weather evenings in the neighborhood playground. Even when I'm racing to the office or keen to get back to my laptop, I stop to check how people are doing, hear their news, and sometimes just hang out. I'll admit that when my kids were very little I initially gravitated to other working mothers, thinking we'd have more in common. But I quickly learned that stay-at-home moms (and dads) could be close friends and amazing allies, too. When you engage with a broad swath of fellow parents, you widen everyone's circle of support.

Offer Your Help

This essay is about getting help, yes, but I recommend giving it first. As Wharton professor Adam Grant has documented, the people who are most successful at building networks and bolstering their careers as a result are those who offer their time, energy, and advice to others without expecting anything in return. Of course, this initial generosity starts a virtuous cycle of reciprocity. When we help people, they instinctively want to help us in return, and vice versa.

How does a busy working parent make time for that? When trying to connect with parents at your school or in your community, it can be as simple as offering to set up a post-practice carpool and handle the first run on an evening when you don't have to work late. Maybe you can't host an after-school playdate, but your sitter could, or you might volunteer to arrange one for the weekend. If your classroom parent is asking for people to contribute food and drinks for the next school get-together, sign up immediately for something easy like juice, napkins, or store-bought bagels.

On snow days in Boston, when schools are closed, my neighborhood friend Melanie, a realtor with three rowdy boys, employs this strategy: She immediately texts every boy mom within a half-mile radius (there are many scattered throughout our city streets) and offers to take their kids for the morning. If she's lucky, someone else—occasionally me—will volunteer for the afternoon. Sometimes, she keeps the crew for the whole day. But if she ever needs someone to babysit while she's showing a house or meeting a client, she has a dozen of us to call on.

At the office, simply treat your fellow working parents the way you would want to be treated. Encourage them to work from home when it makes their family lives easier. Cover for them when they need to leave early or come in late. Notice when they seem to be struggling and ask if there's anything you can do to help. Regularly offer words of encouragement and, when appropriate, advice.

Make the Ask

Many working parents, and particularly working moms, are keen to prove they can do it all. You don't want to seek out special treatment from your boss or colleagues or depend on other parents to take care of your kids. Abandon those notions. Get comfortable asking for help.

The first step is to understand that people like assisting others more than we realize, as psychologist Heidi Grant has noted (see chapter 10, "Too Much to Do? Here's How to Ask for Help"). Often, they don't consider it a burden. In fact, it makes them feel good. Even if you haven't yet initiated the cycle of reciprocity I describe above, don't underestimate how willing most people (particularly fellow parents) are to lend you a hand.

My colleagues know that the best time to schedule meetings with me is during school hours because I've politely asked them to make that accommodation. It's not always possible, but they know I'd like them to try. On the home front, I used to feel guilty about help requests, especially at the last minute, but my posse responds so positively to every ask that I've stopped worrying about it. I send texts like these: "Just left the office so won't make pickup in time. Any chance you could grab E?" "Forgot the sitter is away today. Would you mind taking an extra kid after school?" "Anyone able to give J a ride?" And the answers are always: "Sure!" "No problem!" "I can!"

Learn from Others

My view is that there are no universal rules to follow because each kid, each parent, and each parent–child relationship is unique. But I do firmly believe that we become better working parents when we talk through our problems with others in the same position and listen to and learn from them.

The best piece of working-parent advice I think I've ever received came from my colleague and dear friend, Scott, dad to two girls, five and eight years older than mine. I'd been worrying that, in what little time I had with my kids in the mornings and evenings, I was focused more on discipline than fun. I didn't want them to think of me as someone who was either absentee (when at the office) or a scold (when at home). Scott's response: "It's not your job to be their friend. Your job is to make them better people." I felt instantly reassured and have shared this wisdom with many others.

More recently, I was chatting with a dad whose son and daughter go to school with mine; he's also a pediatric cardiologist. We had a long conversation about middle schools, work, politics, climate change, and health care. He could tell I was stressed about many of these things and at the end of our conversation said something like: "You know, in my job and in the world, there are so many things I can't control. So I try to focus on those things I can."

None of us are dealing with exactly the same issues, but chances are your working-parent friends, in both your professional and personal worlds, have navigated similar ones or know other people who have. So observe them, talk to them, lean on them. These sessions can be impromptu but consider also planning regular check-ins with the inner circle of your posse. Dan and I have had adjoining desks since we started at HBR 10 years ago, and any time we both have a free moment, we make sure to quickly catch up on work and family matters. Similarly, my friend of 20 years, Rebecca, a fellow writer-editor, *Financial Times* alum, and mom of two, and I aim for a weekly lunch, coffee, or walk to discuss what's going on in our lives.

Balancing a career and a family isn't something you must do alone or with only your partner. Create your own parenting posse. There's a reason it's a cliché; we do get by with a little help from our friends.

Adapted from "Working Parents Need a 'Parenting Posse'," on hbr.org, March 4, 2020 (product # H05GEP).

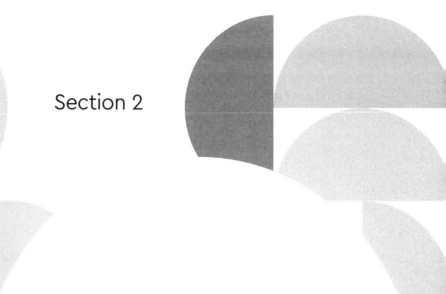

Section 2

Say No to Doing Everything

Put Your Real Priorities First

Does Your Schedule Reflect Your Values?

by Elizabeth Grace Saunders

Quick Takes

Working parents need to be exceptionally intentional with their time. The answer is creating a values-driven schedule.

- Use a values-driven schedule to be more intentional with your time

- Identify what's important—and what isn't

- Define why what's important to you matters

- Identify actions related to your priorities and place them in your calendar

- Discuss your values-driven schedule with those whom it will affect

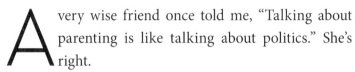

A very wise friend once told me, "Talking about parenting is like talking about politics." She's right.

Because of the highly personal nature of parenting, individuals tend to have strong opinions of the way things "should" be as a working parent. Being pulled in different directions—the expectations from both work and home, and the stress that comes with them—can mean parents struggle with questions like: Can I make it home in time for dinner? Will I be able to help with driving to evening activities? Can I even arrive in time to tuck my kids into bed? How much work travel is too much? Is it OK to take time during the day to exercise if it means leaving before the kids go to school or getting home later? Is it OK for me to see my friends if I feel like I barely get enough time with my family?

As a time management coach, my role is not to critique your parenting style but to encourage you to live a life aligned with your values. Especially as a working parent, that requires you to be exceptionally intentional with your time. Part of that is developing—and living by—a values-driven schedule. A values-driven schedule requires you to determine what is most important to you and your family, and then craft your calendar around those priorities, rather than fitting your family and yourself around whatever might land on your schedule. (See chapter 3, "Sync Up Your Family Calendars.") This helps ensure that you can feel satisfied overall with your time and parenting choices, instead of feeling guilty or frustrated that you're not investing your time in the people and activities that matter most to you.

Here is a three-step process to create a values-driven schedule, based on strategies I've seen be effective for my clients who are working parents.

Step 1: Get Clear on What's Most Important

Begin by listing these key items:

- **The categories you want to include in your schedule:** Consider time for work, family, exercise, learning, social activities, alone time, hobbies, etc.

- **The level of achievement you want in these areas:** Identify your goals and the time commitment required. Going to the gym to work out for 40 minutes three times a week is a different time commitment than training for an Ironman, just as making time to see some of your child's soccer games requires less time than coaching the team. Be realistic about how much time you'll need for each category you've written down.

- **Essential rituals for yourself or your family:** Maybe you want to be home for family dinner at least three nights a week, attend a service at a place of worship each week, and detach from electronics by 10 p.m. so you can connect with your spouse before bed. Jot down these routines and how regularly they should happen.

Your time choices not only impact you but also the other members of your family. As you make this list, have some discussions with your kids and spouse or co-parent about what matters most to them. For example, maybe your son doesn't mind you heading to the office before he gets up, but it would mean the world to him if you leave work in time to see him in his school play.

This is also a really good time to identify what's not important for you to do. Perhaps there are professional organizations where membership would be nice but the decreased time with your family isn't worth the trade-off right now. Or you may have the ability to get outside help with some tasks such as housecleaning, lawn care, errands, or handyman items, so you can use that time working on your side gig or spending time with your kids.

Step 2: Define Why They're Important

Once you have defined your categories, levels of achievement, and essential rituals, think about *why* each one of these is important to you. Go through each one and write down why you believe they are significant.

Thinking about the "why" can strengthen your resolve to follow through. It's one thing to say, "I should exercise," but it's another to frame it as, "I want to exercise because I want to live a long, healthy life where I can be present for my children and my future grandchildren." It can also help you weed out false priorities. For instance, if the strongest reason you can think of for taking a job that will mean 50–75% travel is that it's the usual next step in your career path, step back and think again. Would you love that job? Would it help you fulfill your potential? Would it match your goals? If so, go for it. But if it's just what people usually do but you're not that excited about it, seriously consider whether it's worth that much time away from your family. We often have more options than we think in our jobs, and success comes in many forms.

As you evaluate the "why," look at everything from a 50-year point of view. Think about what you wrote down and ask yourself, "Fifty years from now, what choices would I have been happy that I made? What would matter to me? What wouldn't?" In the moment, things like a work contract can seem so incredibly urgent and important, but over the 50-year span, making (or missing) memories with your family will likely be what you remember.

Step 3: Fuse Your Priorities with Your Schedule

Once you're clear on your priorities, identify related actions and get them in your calendar. This helps to make doing them more automatic and makes it much easier to live a values-driven life.

Start by plugging your essential rituals into your calendar, and then add new items as recurring events based on your priorities. Here are some examples of priorities translated into calendar actions:

- **Exercise:** Go to the gym on Monday, Wednesday, and Friday before work from 6:30–7:30 a.m.

- **Family time:** Eat Saturday morning breakfast with the family around 8 a.m.

- **Connection time:** 15–20 minutes before their bedtime, talk to the kids about anything on their minds. Spend some time talking with my spouse before going to bed as well.

- **Activity time:** Leave at 4:30 p.m. on Tuesdays to take my daughter to dance class.

- **Alone time:** Take a 15-minute walk around 2:30 p.m. to clear my head and get refreshed.

Then have discussions with the people who this might impact about how you can make this work for all of you—and why it's so important. Maybe your spouse helps with getting the kids ready on the mornings when you go work out. Then you return the favor the other days. With your children, there may be days when you need to work late to compensate for the time you took off to take your child to dance class or to participate in another extracurricular activity. But if you explain to them that you want to make time to talk before bed and really follow through on that commitment, that can help them still feel heard and connected. And if your values-based schedule adjustments impact your normal working hours, you may also want to have a discussion with your boss to explain your intentions.

The needs of each family are unique, but the importance of values-based scheduling is universal. I encourage you to take the time to think through these three steps and to create a schedule that reflects your priorities and values so that you'll look back with satisfaction on the choices you made as a working parent.

Adapted from "Working Parents: Does Your Schedule Reflect Your Values?" on hbr.org, November 26, 2019 (product #H05AMY).

Let Go of the Idea of Balance

An *HBR IdeaCast* Interview with
Stewart D. Friedman and Alyssa F. Westring

Quick Takes

- See being a parent as an asset that you can bring to work

- Regain your sense of control by taking a step back and reflecting

- Don't just tell your kids what to do; tell them why it's important

- Find four-way wins for your family

- Be present wherever you are, whether at home or at work

CURT NICKISCH: This is *HBR IdeaCast.* I'm Curt Nickisch. When you try to balance the needs of a partner, children, a demanding boss—and even your own high bar of achievement—it can feel like you are always disappointing someone.

Work and parenting, say today's guests, don't need to be that way. In fact, making key decisions in your career, as a leader at work, can also guide you in the way you parent—and those choices can strengthen all aspects of your life.

Our guests are Stewart Friedman, an organizational psychologist at the Wharton School, and Alyssa Westring, a management professor at the Driehaus College of Business at DePaul University. Together they wrote the book *Parents Who Lead: The Leadership Approach You Need to Parent with Purpose, Fuel Your Career, and Create a Richer Life.*

Stewart and Alyssa, both of you, despite being at different places in your careers and parenting lives, look at parenting as a source of power—that parenting can actually enhance your leadership abilities at work and the other way around. Why do you think of it that way?

ALYSSA WESTRING: I think it's important to see being a parent as an asset that you can bring to work and as something that makes you more fully you, through which you can live your values and bring them to all parts of your life. Feeling proactive is another way of feeling powerful, in that you're not just at the mercy of your situation, that you have the ability to make choices for yourself, and to think about things and to talk about things in a way that doesn't just leave you responding to whichever person—boss, spouse, or child—who puts the most pressure on you.

I think a lot of us want to get out of that space where we're just putting out fires and whichever fire that is burning the brightest is the one we deal with. Our approach invites people to take a step back and to say, "What do I want this to look like? I'm not just reacting to the world that I'm in. How do I take that power that's available to me and use it?" People don't really see that they have that power.

CN: *How do you get that power when you are in a place that you feel like you just have to keep up with everything? Or are there times when you're going to have to give your children more and work less—a lean-out type of job, maybe—and other times when you really have to lean in and maybe get some support from others because you just can't do both? How do you step back from that?*

STEWART FRIEDMAN: Well, it's not easy. Most people go through the daily grind without having anyone to help them take a moment to step back and reflect on who they are and what their purpose is and what their values are and what they stand for and the kind of world that they're trying to create.

What we have found in our work together is that when you help people articulate their values to craft a vision that is shared within the partnership, as well as with others, they feel a greater sense of control because they have a sense of direction and purpose.

CN: *Do you find that they make very different choices once they do that?*

AW: Yeah, we've seen everything ranging from really large changes in life to tiny tweaks.

SF: Some people do make some big changes. But most of the work that people undertake in our program is in smaller steps. Those can be really big in terms of how they affect your mindset, how you feel. What we hear when we talk to people about what's it like being a working parent, they say, overwhelmed, out of control . . .

AW: Stuck, exhausted . . .

SF: . . . isolated, and without enough of a sense of peace and harmony in their lives. So by stepping back—and it's work, it doesn't come free, you've got to take the time to reflect, to talk, to write—you gain a greater sense of control.

CN: *You talk about harmony more than balance, and you even call work-life balance a myth. Explain the difference.*

AW: What it really comes down to is that the idea of balance puts people in this mindset where they can only see the trade-offs and that to be better at work they have to do worse as a parent or give up something in their community life or sleep less. There's nothing inherently wrong with thinking about trade-offs, but when you're stuck in that mindset you fail to see other opportunities to make things better.

SF: When you think win-lose, then somebody is going to lose. And what we help people do is to see the possibility of four-way wins for your family, which means making a change that's within your scope, something that you have control over, that you can do together that's going to make things better for you, for your kids, for your careers, and for your community.

CN: *What are some specific ways you can interact with your children that mirror how you interact with people at work?*

AW: I like to use the example of a micromanager at work who's overseeing every single thing that you do, watching how you spend your time, how you spend your energy, and correcting every little mistake. I think as parents we often default to that same behavior at home—you have to get up, you have to do your homework, you have to do this, you have to do that—and we forget about the why.

At work, a great leader would say: *Here's our vision, Here are our values. Here's why this strategic change is important.* As parents, we forget all of that, and we just say: *Get this done. Get this done. Get this done.* It takes away the fun, but also, for our children, it fails to explain why we're asking these things of them. Why is it important to do your homework? Why, as parents specifically, do we care about the investment that you're making in your community or volunteering? So, it's not just: *Do this; do that.* It's act like a leader as a parent.

To root your interactions with all the people who matter to you, including and especially your children, in what you stand for, what you care about, what your values are, the vision of the world you're trying to create: That's what effective leaders do. That's what parents as leaders do.

CN: *How do you align the goals you have as a parent with the goals you might have at work? It might seem like getting a promotion is totally different from helping your child get over an emotional hurdle.*

SF: One of the families we write about in the book decided to do what they called a "Hike and Pick" experiment, that is, taking some time together, hiking through their neighborhood, and picking up trash. Because the parents had decided that part of what they wanted to convey to their kids—the values that they wanted to transmit through how they were living together and the things they were doing together—was to care for the environment. So they decided to do this on a regular basis, and they felt really good about spending quality time together out there in the world, exercising by walking but also doing something to make their world a little bit better.

CN: *The same way a good leader would not just cut a check to some corporate social responsibility program but actually do something, find out what is meaningful to people in the company, and get more people involved.*

SF: The dad in this case worked in land management, so he knew something about the community and was able to speak to that as part of his experience with his family.

Sometimes it's a matter of simply seeing what you do in a fresh light by shifting the frame on how you think about your work. There was one pharmaceutical executive who came to the realization that what he was doing with his work was creating health. That was something he wanted his family, as well as the people in his organization, to have more top of mind to understand who he was and what he was doing with his work. By conveying this message, creating health for other people became a source of inspiration not just for his organization but also to his family, and that shifted how his kids saw him.

CN: *What do people struggle with as they try to think about leading at home the same way they lead at work?*

AW: I think they struggle the same way people trying to create change at work struggle, which is with a fear of change. *If I shift things*, they think, *they might get worse.* People feel like they have to be perfect, like they have to do everything 100%, like they need to be the best employee and the perfect parent. Letting go of those things or trying to rethink them—it's scary. People grip their old habits more tightly when they think something bad could happen.

When we're working with parents, we're constantly practicing getting comfortable with being uncomfortable. The changes they're making don't have to be permanent. You can try something and it might not work, and you can always go back. Getting people comfortable with taking some calculated, intelligent risks with how they live their lives is a constant in the work that we do.

CN: *Do you have a favorite first step? Or small step? I realize everybody's family and work situation is different, but do you have something that you like to suggest to people if they're just trying to get a sense of where to start?*

AW: One is the idea of being present, being where you are. When you're at work, take a small step to be more focused on what you need to be accomplishing rather than dealing with a hundred different things at once or putting out fires.

Same thing at home. Parents are really worried about how much screen time their kids are getting, but when we ask parents to talk to their kids, the kids are really upset about how much screen time the parents are getting. Think about why you are always on your phone. Could you put it away for even a few minutes to be really in that moment with your kids? You don't need to spend five hours a day having time with your kids if you have 20 minutes of real quality conversation or read them a book, really connecting on a deeper level.

CN: *The same way somebody might go into the office and spend a half hour just thinking to themselves what they need to do to make this a successful week applies to home life. That same kind of good-practice business thinking can be used, where every Sunday night they're just mapping out: What do I need to do for a successful week with the family? Just applying good business lessons at home can yield big results.*

AW: Exactly. We have worked with couples who have a logistics planning meeting on Sunday night, when they go through the calendar and they say: *Here's what's* happening. *Who is going to do what? What are our responsibilities?* It takes the pressure of coordinating everything in the midst of the rest of the week. Just like you would do if you were leading a team, you wouldn't just wait till the moment to lead. You would do it in advance.

CN: *I know families that have used planning and project management software to take care of home stuff. Sometimes people feel sheepish about it because they're like, I'm running my family like a business.*

AW: If you say I'm running my family like a leader who has a tool, maybe that's a slightly different way of thinking about it. It's less cold.

SF: Picking up on the idea of the Sunday night conversation, one family simply did a round with each member of the family talking about the biggest challenge they were facing that week and what help they needed to meet that challenge. Just a 20-, 25-minute conversation over the weekend was a way to create more connection, more love, and support, but also more effectiveness in the different parts of the family members' lives.

Adapted from HBR IdeaCast *episode 734, "Working Parents, Let Go of the Idea of Balance," March 31, 2020.*

How to Spend Your Parenting Time and Energy Wisely

by Amy Jen Su

Quick Takes

To make the best of your finite time and energy as a parent, align your contribution and your passion.

- Determine what you do that your children value the most

- Reflect on which parenting activities motivate and inspire you the most

- Prioritize tasks and experiences that fulfill both of these

- Delegate or spend less time on activities that don't fulfill either

Carole came into our coaching meeting looking especially frustrated. As an IT leader at her company, she was under constant time pressure, and her week had gotten off to a stressful start. "I move mountains to wrap up work early on Tuesdays to get to my teen daughter's soccer practice, only to feel like she doesn't even care I'm there! I don't know what to do. Sometimes, if I don't go, I feel guilty. When I do make the time, I feel underappreciated. It's a no-win situation." This mounting frustration, she shared, had left her distracted and less engaged over the following two days, both at home and at work.

I hear scenarios like this frequently from clients who are working parents. And I have faced them myself. Both at work and as parents, we place high expectations on ourselves to be effective, successful, and to make the best use of our limited time. Misusing that time, in either realm, can feel like a double failure.

Despite the exhaustion of the early years, things are simpler the younger our children are. Newborns' needs can be summed up in a short list beginning with food, care, and love—and we do it all. As they start school and advance through their teen years, our ability to find our highest and best use as parents becomes more complex. As we juggle work and home, with our time always squeezed, how can we ensure that we are spending our parenting time and energy in the right ways, especially as our children age and change? It begins with two questions.

Define Your Contributions and Passions as a Parent

Instead of ending up feeling underappreciated or guilty about the time you do or don't spend with your kids, you can proactively triage your parenting time and energy. I recommended that Carole try an approach I use with leaders at work: prioritizing according to contribution and passion. To do this, think of one of your children and answer the following questions:

1. **Contribution:** Which of the activities I do, tasks I perform, or types of support I provide does my child value the most right now? (Answer for each child you have individually.)

2. **Passion:** Which activities, tasks, or types of support give me the most motivation, inspiration, or energy as a parent?

TABLE 8-1

Parenting time 2×2

		Contribution	
		Low	High
Passion	**High**	**Q3: Low/High** Deemphasize activities that may be outdated and are no longer as relevant or of high value to your child.	**Q1: High/High** Prioritize activities where contribution to your child and your passion match.
	Low	**Q4: Low/Low** Eliminate or delegate to the extent possible.	**Q2: High/Low** Manage the energy impact. Ask for help or delegate where possible.

Determine Parenting Time and Stay Relevant Using a 2×2

You can take the two criteria above and create a corresponding 2×2 set of quadrants to help guide decisions around parenting time (see table 8-1).

Quadrant 1: High contribution/High passion

This is the sweet spot of parenting time, as these activities add value for your child and give you an energy boost. As Carole looked at her answers to the questions, she realized her best times with her daughter included activities where she both contributed and from which she derived passion, including their mutual interest in technology, going for runs together, or researching things her daughter was interested in. These are the activities where parents and children truly bond. She agreed to start prioritizing her parenting time for things that fell in quadrant 1.

Quadrant 2: High contribution/Low passion

Activities in quadrant 2 can be tricky as our kids will have needs that may drain our energy. The answer isn't to stop doing them but to minimize their energy impact or identify resources that can provide help. For example, Carole realized that she was tired after filling out school forms, but that this was something that her husband didn't mind doing. They compared their contributions and passions and looked for places where her quadrant 2 matched his quadrant 1 and vice versa. Working parents who have a caregiver can optimize their resources further.

Quadrant 3: Low contribution/High passion

Our kids' interests and needs are always changing. Quadrant 3 is a real danger zone for parents because often we find ourselves engaging with our kids around activities or interests we love but our kids don't actually value.

Even worse, we risk putting inadvertent pressure on our children to engage in an activity because they know we care about it as the parent.

Therefore, it is critical to set up regular checkpoints with our kids to understand how they regard our contributions as they age. As a working parent myself, I use a ritual each year where I sit down with my son at the start of each school year and ask him the top three things I do as a mom that he values the most. When he was younger, I made a list of all the things we did together and had him put a star next to his favorite three items. Now that he is older, it's a much more open-ended conversation. Then, to find the sweet spot, I line up his top three contributions against my top three passions.

It's been amazing for me to see how this sweet spot of time for us has evolved through the years. When he was younger, even when we had a nanny, he most valued and I most enjoyed doing a certain number of drop-offs or pickups from school during the week, attending a karate practice, and tucking him in at bedtime. As a teen now, he doesn't value and in fact doesn't want me to be seen at school drop-off or pickup! Instead, he values my time at key volleyball tournaments on the weekends, especially the ones out of town.

By staying in tune with who he is now, versus being grounded in the past, I am better able to ensure staying in quadrant 1 versus quadrant 3.

Quadrant 4: Low contribution/Low passion

When things are busy or when you try to do everything, you can end up engaged on autopilot in activities that neither add value nor bring you passion. It is easy for parents to fall into habits and assumptions and continue doing what they have always done without reconsideration. This can lead to frustrating moments like the one Carole experienced at her daughter's soccer practice. She was used to going to her daughter's practice on Tuesdays, even though it turned out that this didn't bring value or energy for either of them anymore.

If you find yourself in quadrant 4, it's best to stop doing those activities that are no longer relevant for you or your child and gain back precious time.

Operationalize into Your Calendar

Learning the quadrants is only the first step. If you don't have a plan for putting your insights into action, your good intentions to spend time with your kids in the best ways will get swept up in your long list of to-dos. Use your calendar to carve out and protect time for quadrant 1 activities (see chapter 6, "Does Your Schedule Reflect Your Values?").

Use pre-blocks

Pre-block your calendar with major school events like performances or teacher conferences as soon as that information is available. It's not perfect, and there will be plenty of weeks where work travel or deliverables get in the way, but proactively planning will enable you to have an honest discussion ahead of time when you can't be there.

Color-code

Color-coding your calendar can help you take a longer view of how you spend your time. Carole highlighted any quadrant 1 time she spent with her daughter in orange. It helped her to see the trend line over a longer arc of time versus expecting herself to be perfectly balanced in any given week. Color-coding is not intended to make you feel guilty (as working parents often do), but rather to serve as a cue to adapt as needed.

Stay in Active Dialogue

Even with the best of triaging or planning time with your kids, it is important to stay in active conversation with them to keep them involved and adapt to changes.

Use look-aheads

Throughout the year, bring your family together to see what is upcoming on the calendar. For families with older children, you can designate a day and time such as Sunday morning at breakfast to have everyone pull up laptops and calendars, and scan for the upcoming week. Especially with multiple kids, where sibling rivalry over parents' time and attention can exist, the family look-ahead can help to ensure that parenting time is distributed fairly.

For younger children, use visuals such as wall calendars or large whiteboards with pictures denoting when you have work or other obligations. Often, the uncertainty and inconsistency of when you will or won't be home are what kids struggle with the most.

Talk about it

Talking to our kids regularly about where and how we spend our time gives us a chance to model good communication and time management practices. If the amount of time you are (or aren't) spending with children is a road bump in your family's progress, have a conversation rather than avoiding it or letting things fester. Ask your kids to be active problem solvers with you in finding more satisfying ways to spend time together. Let them see you ask for help from other family members, neighbors, or your spouse when you get into a time bind.

Ultimately, Carole felt much more in control and effective as she became intentional around her parenting time decisions. Carole and her daughter collaboratively agreed that Carole should stop leaving work early for soccer practices. Instead, her daughter encouraged her to use that time she was at practice to focus on work and then come to pick her up afterward. Her daughter shared that, as a teen, what she valued now was the car time after practice, when they could talk and catch up one-on-one on each other's day with few distractions.

• • •

My hope for myself and all working parents like Carole is that the practices outlined in this article will help us find new confidence in the ways we spend our time and alleviate guilt about letting go of some things we simply don't have enough time to do. These changes can increase our fulfillment at work and help maintain meaningful relationships with our kids as they grow up.

"Delegating with Joy"

A *Women at Work* Interview with Tiffany Dufu

Quick Takes

- Release yourself from unrealistic expectations

- Stop "imaginary delegation"

- Learn to delegate with joy

- Put your energy to your highest and best use

SARAH GREEN CARMICHAEL: *This is* Women at Work. *I'm Sarah Green Carmichael. In 2008 Tiffany Dufu had a high-powered job dedicated to getting more women into government. She was also raising a 2-year-old with her husband. Then, during the Great Recession her husband got laid off. Tiffany became the sole breadwinner as well as the meal planner, childcare expert, and life organizer. It was all too much, and one day she came home to find her out-of-work husband watching basketball on the couch. "What's for dinner?" he asked. Overwhelmed, she screamed back, "You tell me!" It was a turning point in their relationship and her career and started a series of conversations between the two of them over what it* really *meant to have it all.*

As they started to figure it out together, Tiffany began to do the kind of ruthless delegating and time protecting that most women think isn't possible. And she noticed that although she wanted to talk to other women about her life's work, getting more women into leadership roles, women kept asking her for advice on how to get more done in less time. She realized the two would have to go together, so she wrote a book about it called Drop the Ball: Achieving More *by Doing Less. Nicole Torres and I talked with her about how she's helping other woman to not get lost in their work.*

NICOLE TORRES: *So, what is the advice that you now give to other women?*

TIFFANY DUFU: Well, I definitely tell them to drop the ball. I used to be someone who was terrified of ever dropping a ball. If I did, it meant to me that I was failing to take timely action. I was disappointing myself. I was disappointing the other people in my life who loved me in my particular place. I was disappointing the entire black race, which sounds dramatic, but that is actually how it felt.

I decided to reappropriate the term. For me, dropping the ball means releasing these unrealistic expectations that all of us face, no matter who we are, about who we should be. It means figuring out what really matters most to you and what your highest and best use is, and meaningfully engaging the people in your life to support you in your journey. My biggest piece of advice is, first of all, just figure out what matters to you most.

SGC: *Part of dropping the ball is not just that things don't get done; it's that you have to delegate them to other people, right? And in the book you talk about the* *trap of imaginary delegation, and it struck me that, oh my God, that's what I'm doing wrong! So, tell us about that.*

TD: Imaginary delegation is this phenomenon where you assign someone a task, and you fully expect them to complete the task, and when they don't, you become annoyed, sometimes even angry . . . but you never actually tell them verbally that you assigned the task to them. And then when common sense prevails and you say to yourself, "You know, I never actually told him to take out the recycling," you quickly snap back at common sense, "Well, nobody has to tell *me* to take out the recycling around here." If you're someone who ever walks into your home or your office and thinks to yourself, "Am I the only person who can see that X, Y, or Z needs to be done?" you're probably doing a little bit of imaginary delegating. And I used imaginary delegation for a long time to try to engage people in my life, especially my husband, to do things to support me. And you know, it just doesn't work because people don't know what's inside of your head. So I had to learn how to not only stop imaginary delegating, but then figure out to delegate with joy to really get the support that I needed.

SGC: *Explain that. How do you delegate with joy—do you just have to accept that you need to be the delegator?*

Because I do run into that, like you say, that it's Wednesday night, the recycling always goes out Wednesday night, I shouldn't have to ask anyone else to do it.

TD: It's really tough because in the world that we live in, it's not fair, but women are socially conditioned to tie their value to things like whether or not the recycling is taken out. And men are not. So that's part of the reason why women see those things. But the other piece of this is if there is something that is happening in your home on a regular basis that you're not responsible for, sometimes it can be invisible to you too.

So I created a list of all the things that were required in order for us to manage our home. The idea was for my husband and me to divide the responsibilities on the list between the two of us. But instead, he wanted to add more to the list, and I couldn't imagine what could possibly be added to the list, since I was the one who did everything and I knew what was on the list. As it turns out, there were a number of things, like watering plants. It dawned on me: You know, they are alive, and I never water them. So those kinds of experiences help you to understand that taking out the recycling is in your column and you see that, but it really would require an act on your part to help other people see it. Delegating with joy is just putting a task and an ask in a much higher context, a more important context than just being a chore.

I started delegating with joy with just two things that I needed my husband to do, which seems so small, but it was such a big deal to me. To begin, I did what I would do at work: I scheduled. I picked a time that didn't conflict with any sporting event, because he's addicted to pretty much every sport, and I sat him down, and I said, "Hey, I want to talk to you.

"Lately I've been really stressed, and I feel like it's having a negative impact on our relationship and my ability to do really amazing things in the world. And I've been doing a lot of thinking. I figured out what matters most to me, and I feel like there's a bunch of things that I'm doing that don't really ladder up to that. And you are my biggest cheerleader and my biggest champion, and I know that we started this journey together because we committed to supporting one another, and I was wondering, in the interest of helping me figure out how to be my best self, if you could do a couple of things. And when I tell you what they are, you're going to be like, 'Why didn't you just send me a text message? Why are you giving me this big speech?' But babe, that's how important these two things are to me. One is that you take out the recycling and the other is that you pick up the dry cleaning."

SGC: *There you go. You start small and build on success. The book is full of great advice. Do you ever struggle to follow your own excellent advice?*

TD: Oh, all the time. Every day. [LAUGHTER] Yeah, we're all on a journey. I do have some practices that help me tremendously. For example I have a "drop the ball" question that I ask myself multiple times a day, especially when I've got a lot of emails in my inbox and a lot of deadlines, which is basically "Will responding to this email or answering this phone call or saying yes to this committee put me to my highest and best use in achieving the things that matter most to me, which are having a really healthy partnership, raising my children as conscious global citizens, and advancing women and girls?" And if the answer is yes, I'm like, OK, let me stop and just figure out how I might be able to make this happen. But most of the time the answer is no, and I move on. There are consequences to dropping the ball, but I certainly move on knowing that I'm doing what I need to do in order to create a life that I'm passionate about.

Adapted from Women at Work *episode 6, "The Advice We Get and Give,"* *March 8, 2018.*

Too Much to Do? Here's How to Ask for Help

by Heidi Grant

Quick Takes

- Admit that you need to ask for help more often (i.e., "ask for help more often")

- Figure out exactly what you need

- Ask for it directly and clearly

- Accept the help that you are offered

- Say thank you

Raise your hand if you have an insurmountable pile of projects on your to-do list and an inbox so terrifying to behold that you can hardly bear to behold it.

Cue the sea of arms waving wildly.

You have too much to do. You can't do it alone. You need people to help you. *Why aren't they helping you?!?*

Here's the uncomfortable truth: If you aren't getting the support you need with your crushing workload, odds are it's kind of your fault.

Cue the sea of angry readers making an obscene gesture at me right now.

What I mean is, you probably aren't asking for the support you actually need, and if you *are*, you probably aren't asking for it in the right way. Loads of studies have found that people have an innate desire to be helpful, by and large. (This is one reason the "givers" among us tend to get overwhelmed.) But even though people are much more likely to lend us a hand than we assume, most of us can't stand the idea of asking for help.[1]

If you're drowning in work and other tasks right now, you need to get over your aversion to asking for help. Try the following steps:

Figure Out What You Actually Need

First, set aside time to figure out what, specifically, would *really* help you.

People who are drowning aren't always at their most rational and strategic. We may neglect to ask for help because we can't even make sense of what to ask *for*. And the last thing we want to do is stop and think about it—better to push ahead, alone and stressed to the point of breaking.

Just as they say you have to spend money to make money, the truth is you sometimes have to spend a little time in order to save a lot of it. So take a moment to go through everything on your plate. Identify tasks that someone could help you with that meet both of the following criteria:

- Having someone do it for you would provide significant relief or make you substantially more effective.

- Someone could do it for you without needing tons of supervision or explaining.

Ask for It—Very Clearly

One of the most underestimated obstacles to *giving* help is uncertainty. No one wants to offer unwanted help—

people tend to get cranky when you do. If someone is unsure about whether you want help, how to help, or whether they can give you what you need, they aren't going to help you.

It's common for people who need to ask for help to be vague in how they ask for it, out of an aversion to the whole situation. Social psychologists have found, over and over, that asking for help fills us with intense discomfort—even, sometimes, a physical revulsion. And so we end up couching our request for help as a question ("Would you like to . . . ?") or a favor ("If you have time . . ."). This leads to uncertainty, which leads to inertia.

It's up to *you* to take all that uncertainty away by:

- Making an explicit request for help

- Being very, very specific about what it is you want them to do, and when

- Being careful to choose someone who actually *can* help in the way you are asking

Accept Whatever Help You Are Offered

There are two ways in which we all tend to be overly rigid when it comes to accepting help, both of which can be self-defeating.

The first is being rigid about *the type of help* we are looking for. For example, I was doing research on a book and asked an acquaintance for assistance. He replied that he couldn't spare the time himself, but he offered a different type of help: an introduction to a few colleagues who might be able to lend a hand instead. I ultimately got exactly what I needed from one of those colleagues. The introduction, even though it wasn't what I asked for, was very helpful.

The second has to do with *whom we ask* for help. We all have a tendency to write off the people who have turned down our requests for help in the past. But the research on this one is very clear: People who have rejected your request for help in the past are actually more likely to assist you the second time you ask.[2] This comes, more often than not, from a desire to repair the relationship that might have been damaged by the rejection—and, frankly, from not wanting to look like the kind of jerk who turns someone down twice. So don't hesitate to reach out to the people who have left you high and dry in the past—they may welcome a shot at redemption.

It's important to respect the fact that you haven't cornered the market on drowning in tasks—other people may be swamped too. This is not a reason *not* to ask; it's a reason to be flexible about the help you are offered and from whom.

Say Thank You

Really, this last step should go without saying, but you can't take anything for granted these days. One of the most important motivators for helpers is the potential to feel effective. Studies show that when people can vividly imagine the impact their help will have—or, even better, can learn about the *actual* impact it had—they are more motivated to continue helping in the future.[3] Everyone wants to see their help land. It's up to you to make sure they do.

While these steps sound easy, I know they're not—if they were, you wouldn't be drowning in work in the first place. But remember, when it comes to getting the help you need, you have far better chances for success than you realize—if you'll only ask for it.

Adapted from "Drowning in Work? Here's How to Ask a Colleague for Help," on hbr.org, June 14, 2018 (product #H04ECF).

How to Say No to Taking on More

by Rebecca Knight

Quick Takes

- Evaluate whether you have the desire and time to help
- Inquire if there are smaller ways to pitch in
- Practice saying "no" out loud
- Be kind but firm
- Be honest and make sure your "no" is understood

Editor's Note: This article was written about politely and effectively saying "no" to taking on more work at work—and working parents need to have this skill down cold. But these techniques are just as essential for declining some of the countless requests parents face from their children's schools, sports, clubs, and activities. Whether it's being asked to be treasurer of the parent-teacher association, assistant coaching your toddler's soccer team, or delivering brownies to yet another bake sale, the advice in this article will help you keep your workload outside of work under control and allow you to devote more time and energy to your highest priorities.

Sometimes you have too much on your plate or you're just not interested in taking on a project or role you've been offered. You might not have a choice in the matter, but if you do, how do you turn down the opportunity in a way that won't offend the person offering? How can you avoid being labeled "not a team player" or "difficult to work with"?

What the Experts Say

For most of us, saying "no" doesn't come naturally. You feel lousy disappointing a colleague, guilty about turning down your boss, and anxious denying a client's request. "You don't want to be seen as a 'no person,'" says Karen Dillon, coauthor of *How Will You Measure Your Life?* "You want to be viewed as a 'yes person,' a 'go-to person'—a team player." Trouble is, agreeing to work on too many assignments and pitching in on too many projects leaves you stretched and stressed. Saying "no" is vital to both your success and the success of your organization—but that doesn't make it any easier to do, says Holly Weeks, the author of *Failure to Communicate.* "People say, 'There is no good way to give bad news.' But there are steps you can take to make the conversation go as well as possible." Here are some pointers.

Take some time to assess the request

Before you respond with a knee-jerk "no," Dillon advises assessing the request first by determining how "interesting, engaging, and exciting the opportunity is," and then by figuring out whether it's feasible for you to help. "Think about what's on your plate, whether priorities can be shuffled, or whether a colleague could step in to assist you [on your other projects]," she says. "Don't say 'no' until you're sure you need to." The assessment ought not be a solo endeavor, adds Weeks. She suggests providing the person who's making the request—be it a client, a coworker, or your manager—with context about your workload so he can "help you evaluate the scale and scope" of what he's asking. You need to know, for instance, "Is this a small thing that won't take too long? Or is it a longer-term project? And how important is it?" She says the goal is for you to understand "how much your saying 'no' is going to cost the other person" and for your counterpart to grasp the "repercussions of what he's asking."

Be straightforward with your response

If you realize you have neither the desire nor the bandwidth to help and, therefore, need to turn down the request, be honest and up front about your reasons, advises Weeks. "Too often people start with lightweight reasons and hold back the real reason they're saying 'no' because they think it's too heavy," she says. "But the little, self-deprecating explanations are not persuasive and are easily batted aside. Or they come across as disingenuous." To limit frustration, be candid about why you're saying "no." If you're challenged, stay steady, clear, and on message. Dillon recommends describing your workload and the "projects on your plate" by saying something like, "I would be unable to do a good job on your project, and my other work would suffer."

Offer a lifeline

To maintain a good relationship with the person you're turning down, it's critical to "acknowledge the other side," says Weeks. Be empathetic. Be compassionate. She suggests saying something like: "'I realize that by saying "no," this [chore] is going to be put back in your hands.' The other person might not be happy with your answer, but he will be able to tolerate it." Dillon suggests offering a lifeline by asking if there "are small ways you can be helpful" to the project. Perhaps you can attend brainstorming sessions, read first drafts, or simply serve as a sounding board. Even in saying "no," you want to "convey team spirit," she says. If you're unable to offer small favors, be sure to keep optics in mind. "If you're saying you're too busy to help, don't cut out early and don't be seen taking long, chatty breaks at the watercooler."

Be kind but firm

"The manner in which you say 'no' is so important," says Dillon. "Don't make the other person feel bad for asking you for help." No sighing, no grimacing, no it's-not-my-turn-why-don't-you-ask-Donna? "Be kind, but firm."

Watch your tone and your body language, says Weeks. Don't shuffle your feet and "don't use facial expressions to express reluctance or demurral." Strive for a neutral "no." It's also vital that you don't leave your counterpart with false hope that your "no" could eventually turn into "yes," she adds. "There is tremendous temptation to soften the 'no' to get a better response," she says. "But when your 'no' is reluctant, flexible, and malleable, it gives the impression of 'maybe I'll change my mind,' and it encourages your counterpart to keep pushing." At the same time, she says, it's reasonable to state that while the answer may be "no" today, things could change in the future.

Adjust your expectations

Even if you follow all the steps above, you should prepare for negative feedback. Your colleague or client "may not be happy; he may punish you or be perfectly content to burn a bridge," says Weeks. "You can influence how the other person reacts, but you can't control it." She suggests "adjusting your expectations" on what you hope to accomplish. You can't please everyone. "Don't look at it as a choice between confrontation and preserving a relationship," she says. Dillon agrees, noting that you shouldn't read too much into the help-seeker's initial reaction. "He feels frustrated. But it may not be personal. Don't assume he's going to be mad at you for three weeks."

Practice

To get better at saying "no," Dillon suggests practicing saying it out loud—either alone, behind closed doors, or with a trusted friend or colleague. "Listen to yourself," she says. Your tone should be clear and your demeanor diplomatic. "You want to say 'no' in a way that makes people respect you." Saying "no" is a skill you can learn, and eventually it'll become easier, adds Weeks. "Think of all the people who have to say 'no' for a living—lawyers, cops, referees, judges," she says. "They do it with dignity. They own what they're saying. And they are accountable for it regardless of strong feelings on both sides."

Adapted from "How to Say No to Taking on More Work," on hbr.org, December 29, 2015 (product #H02KS1).

Getting It All (Mostly) Done

Productivity Tips and Hacks You Need

12

Working from Home When You Have Kids

by Daisy Dowling

Quick Takes

- Keep a routine, but stay flexible in the ways that matter to you

- Broadcast the business benefits of you working from home

- Maintain your professionalism

- Explain the benefits and limits to your kids

- Recognize that working remotely is a skill that's built over time

You're working remotely. Maybe it's due to the structure of your new job or organization; maybe it's part of that new corporate work/life initiative; or maybe it's the result of months of lobbying the higher-ups. Or maybe, like so many parents, you've been thrust unexpectedly—unwillingly, even—into a work-from-home arrangement because of a broader crisis. Remote work is supposed to be all upside: no commute, no office distractions, no one looking disapprovingly at you when you duck out of the office for a pediatrician's appointment. Just you, a comfortable home office, and the opportunity to spend more time with your kids.

Those benefits, however, come with an equivalent number of challenges. How do you stay on the senior leader radar screen when not physically around your colleagues? In a 24-7, always-on work culture, how do you avoid the perception—particularly among more senior or traditionally minded colleagues—that you're slowing down or have chosen the "parent track"? How do you establish constructive workplace relationships with people you see infrequently? How do you avoid the distractions and interruptions that can compromise your performance?

Savvy working parents know that it takes more than a home office to make remote work work for their organizations, careers, and families: It takes conscious effort and some specific, effective tactics—which you can start using today.

When making a case, frame it in business terms. Regardless of the actual reason, successful remote-working parents always present the arrangement in a commercial, good-for-business frame (see chapter 17, "Winning Support for Flexible Work"). "Eliminating my commute frees up seven more hours per week I can spend reaching out to clients" or "My being in Chicago allows the company to cover the Midwest markets efficiently and at no additional cost" are more compelling, inarguable statements than "I wanted to spend more time at home." Present yourself as aligned to revenues and your setup as a corporate asset, and you'll find even the most skeptical colleagues become supportive.

Keep a firm routine. After years of office life, working remotely can feel wonderfully flexible: Get to your desk at 9:30 a.m. in your pajamas! Feed the baby while on the conference call! But that same lack of traditional workplace boundaries has the potential to erode your motivation and productivity (are you really at your best getting a late start, in sweatpants?). Use your remote work setup to create flexibility that's meaningful to you, but keep a firm schedule and habits, too. Start work at the same time each day. Wear what makes you feel sharp and confident. Limit breaks to the same length and frequency as in the office. With a solid routine and the right "guardrails" in place, you'll maximize the feeling of being professional and in control.

Demonstrate your commitment. What your colleagues can't see, they can't appreciate. When working remotely, take care to provide small, clear signals that your commitment and work ethic are unwavering. Key tips: Send emails first thing in the morning as a means of announcing that you're already up and at it. Let colleagues know that you've read their emails and documents carefully: "Brad, Thanks for this—the data on page 6 will be helpful in our quarterly review process." Take calls in the early morning or late at night as a favor to coworkers in other time zones. These small tactics will make you appear eager, committed, and hardworking—good attributes at any level.

Set up your physical work environment. Arrange it to help you be, and be seen as, professional, focused, and committed. Find a way to ensure privacy during critical phone calls. If you're not certain of privacy during critical calls, alert the people you're speaking with that there may be toddler interruptions. Create a professional backdrop for video calls so that no one has to see your kids' ice hockey equipment in the background when you're discussing the quarterly marketing report. Taking charge of these small logistics enhances your working environment and your professional image.

Do a technology audit. Smart use of technology can maximize your efficiency and your connection to colleagues. If you're emailing and calling while everyone else at the office is on Slack, you're missing a real opportunity. Partner with IT, or with a tech-savvy teammate in your department, to help you find and start using the best technological tools. Don't know the best apps for staying in touch and "in the flow" with your company, industry, or function? Ask around to find out.

Allocate 10% of your time to relationship building. In a regular office environment, relationships occur organically—through conversations at the watercooler, in the hallway, at lunch. But when you're working remotely, you will have to create those "connection opportunities" yourself. Call a colleague to check in on their weekend. Email a mentee to ask how her big presentation went. Ensuring that you have regular, informal touch points with everyone on the team—and throughout the organization—will pay big long-term dividends.

Be positively unpredictable. Even if your remote-work arrangement allows for five days a week at home, get into the office every few weeks. Show up for the annual marketing review even if there's a dial-in. Be on hand the week the new recruits start so that you can help mentor and onboard them. You don't have to be present all the time to be present visibly—and when it matters.

Sell your boss. In most organizations, remote work is seen as an employee benefit—and it's always a good idea to share what benefits it's bringing to your boss and the organization in return. So provide your manager with regular, positive reminders as to why your remote arrangement is working and appreciated. "Working from home has let me spend more time on client work. My sell-through rate is up 10% this year—and the fact that the company is providing this flexibility makes me want to be on this team for the long term."

Explain it to your kids. Children may have difficulty understanding the world of work—what it consists of, what it requires, and what it means. But even very small children can hear that "Mommy works hard all week at the office because I like it, and because it lets me earn money to take care of our family. On Fridays, I still work, but from home so that I can take you to school and we can do fun things together." In doing so, you transmit the values of hard work and responsibility—while showing your commitment and love.

• • •

Big picture: Working remotely is a distinct professional skill. As with any other professional skill—like public speaking or negotiations or financial analysis—it's built over time and through experience, personal reflection, desire for continual improvement, and a lot of hard work. And for any working parent who wants to drive organizational performance, succeed on the job, and raise terrific kids, it's a skill well worth developing.

Adapted from "How to Work from Home When You Have Kids," on hbr.org, September 14, 2017 (product #H03W0V).

13

You Can Make Family Meals Happen

by Daisy Dowling

Quick Takes

- Recast your expectations of what a "family meal" is to take pressure off yourself

- Use tricks and planning to shave off shopping and prep time

- Involve your kids

- Try family breakfast if dinner doesn't work for your family

- Keep meals fun, friendly, and brief

As a working parent, it's one of the questions you dread most. And it comes every day, right around 3 p.m.: *"So, umm . . . what are we doing about dinner?"*

Whether the question comes in a text from your partner, teens at home, or it pops into your head during the marketing meeting, you reflexively cringe, because dinnertime is one of the danger zones of working parenthood, when the strains of your dual role feel the most acute.

Why? Because what presents as a straightforward, practical problem—meal prep—is actually a psychological, emotional, and even physical one, too, and it hits working parents when we're the most vulnerable. Exhausted at the end of a long workday and overwhelmed by everything else we have to do, it's easy to turn to restaurant meals and convenience-food options—which, let's face it, won't do your health any favors.

It may feel impossible to get everyone eating at the same time and around the same table. And when you haven't seen your toddler for nine hours, you probably don't have the heart to fight with her over the need to eat broccoli. You *wish* the whole family could close out your days with regular, proper, happy, nutritious, sit-down meals, but instead your nightly experience leaves you feeling conflicted, stressed, and guilty. And you're not alone: Many if not most working parents are caught in the same struggle.

Fortunately, there's a better way forward. By taking a broad-spectrum approach to the problem and by using simple, specific tactics—13 of the most powerful are below—you can go a long way in taming the logistics, reducing your sense of strain, and making more family meals happen.

Seeing—and Taking Charge of— the Big Picture

Make it a priority. It's essential to finish the budget report, get the car repaired, prepare for the big client meeting, make your daughter's school-play costume . . . and on and on and on. Your calendar is crammed, your to do-list a mile long, and a lot of what's on there is marked "urgent." If you're going to make family dinner happen, you need to give it equal priority. This may involve a mindset shift and seeing family meals as a critical part of your routine (in case you need any additional convincing on that front, check out the scientific studies demonstrating that kids who eat with their parents are much less likely to later suffer from substance abuse[1]). A simple, practical step can also help: On your Outlook or Google calendar, block off not just the evening hours you want to eat with the family, but the time for grocery shopping and food prep. When they're recorded as "official" entries, you're much more likely to actually get them done.

Keep it real—and take the pressure off. Chances are, when you think "family dinner" you imagine hearty, hot, home-cooked meals, served nightly and on actual china. Recast your expectations and take some of that pressure off. Maybe you commit to gathering for a meal once a week: every Friday evening, for example. Or maybe it's a family breakfast instead of dinner, if school and work schedules make that easier. And it's fine if the meal itself involves the microwave, leftovers, or paper plates. Perfection isn't the point here. The point is to eat together—regularly.

Set new rules. Your 5-year-old refuses vegetables, your 7-year-old wants the pasta without the sauce . . . or they're both demanding cold cereal instead of what you've served. But your dual role as a working parent is hard enough without also acting as a short-order cook or diplomatic negotiator—so resign those jobs today and set some hard-and-fast new rules. *Everyone gets the same meal: no substitutes and no changes. If you choose not to eat what's served at this meal, you can wait for the next* *one. If you complain, you do the dishes.* Setting—and sticking to—this new regime won't be easy, but if you take a firm stance, meals will be easier and more pleasant from here on out.

Conquering the Food Part

Be ready. It will be impossible to produce any meal, particularly under time pressure, if you don't already have basic kitchen supplies at home. Need a list? Turn to the *New York Times*'s Modern Pantry page and stock up on everything in the section marked "Essentials."

Save time wherever you can. As a working parent, time is your scarcest asset, and if you're trying to squeeze family meals into your already-packed schedule, you need to be super-efficient. So buy fruits and vegetables precut. Put food staples on Amazon automatic reorder. Try a grocery-delivery service. (Yes, these things can be expensive—but they're much cheaper than ordering in.) And as soon as you get home—before you even take your coat off or throw your laptop bag down in the corner— turn on the stove or put a pot of water on a burner. What are you going to bake or boil? Who knows! But by the time you get the kids situated and yourself back in the kitchen, you'll be ready to start cooking.

Practice strategic snacking. If you're starving when you leave work or the kids are when you get home, it will be alluring to reach for the take-out menu, fast food, or other similar options. Instead, keep some nonperishable snacks (dried fruit, raw nuts) in your work bag and in the car, and set some healthy hors d'oeuvres (carrot sticks and hummus, low-fat cheese) out while you're cooking. This will tide everyone over until you can enjoy your main meal calmly and together.

Use the "add healthy" approach. If you're running late from work and decide to get takeout burgers from the fast food drive-through on the way home, don't beat yourself up. Sure, it's not your finest culinary or nutritional moment, but we're dealing in reality here. And there's a way to make things better: Serve up the takeout with some carrot sticks, oranges, and glasses of milk and suddenly you've got a meal long on vitamins A, C, and calcium. Add healthy—and lose the guilt.

Give everyone a job. The more each family member contributes to the family meal, the more likely they are to enjoy it, take pride in it, and feel that it's *theirs*. While you're preparing dinner, have your preschooler put the paper napkins on the table or have your middle schooler toss the salad. Or let the kids prepare the meal themselves. For a little inspiration, show them the *20 Recipes Kids Should Know*—an easy, how-to cookbook written by a 12-year-old (the photos were taken by her high-school-age sister). If a 12-year-old can write a fantastic cookbook, your 10-year-old can follow it.

Have a go-to emergency meal. An omelet and salad. A frozen burrito and a piece of fruit. A bag of frozen vegetables cooked in the same water the pasta is and served with sauce from a jar. It doesn't matter what your *five-minutes-until-it's-ready, I-know-the-kids-will-eat-it* meal is, but be sure to have one. It will help you out in pinch, and you'll feel more in control with a family meal fallback.

Making Your Time at the Table More Powerful—and Enjoyable

Label it. Call it whatever you want—"family dinner," "our family meal," "eating in the dining room," or "sitting down together, all five of us"—but call it *something* and be consistent. The label sends signals about the meal's meaning and importance, and it makes even the simplest and quickest dinner feel like part of a larger family tradition.

Focus on behaviors as much as food. You don't have to set the table with separate meat and fish forks, or expect your 4-year-old to use a finger bowl, but you can use family mealtimes as a way to teach and underscore the importance of respect and manners. Encourage the kids to wait until everyone's seated to eat, to not interrupt someone telling a story, to use their napkins, and to thank the person who passes them the ketchup. Think of life at the family table as preparation for adulthood.

Keep it happy. For the family meal to *work*, it needs to feel like a shelter from the experiences of the day and like a reward instead of a task. So keep things positive: Use this time to share any good news—about weekend plans, for example, or an upcoming visit from Grandma—and start comments with upbeat lead-ins like "the funniest thing happened today . . . ." And no interrogating the kids about yesterday's geometry test—let them decide what they want to talk about.

Keep it brief. For children of any age, end-of-day events can be tough. They're tired, they have shorter attention spans than adults do, and good behavior fades fast. But family meals don't need to be long to have impact. It's their regularity and quality that count. When starting your new routine, aim for just 15 minutes around the table. That timing will naturally lengthen as your kids grow—and as the practice of connecting over shared meals becomes an essential, treasured habit for every member of the family.

Adapted from "How Working Parents Can Make Family Meals Happen," on hbr.org, May 27, 2019 (product #H04YXM).

14

Getting Things Done While Locked Down with Your Kids

Contributed by 18 HBR readers

Quick Takes

- Set boundaries for your kids and for yourself
- Carve out dedicated time for focus
- Let go of screen guilt
- Get extended family involved
- Embrace good enough
- Play, laugh, and be present

Editors' Note: A few months into the Covid-19 pandemic lockdown, we reached out to working parents on HBR's LinkedIn Group and asked them to share advice about how they were getting things done in these impossible circumstances. Great ideas flowed in by hundreds from around the globe, and we've collected a few of our favorites here. While we hope against hope that the pandemic has passed by the time you are reading this book, many of these tips and tricks will be just as valuable in the new normal.

Stagger your day

My husband and I both work from home, and we stagger the times we wake up. I wake up early in the morning while the baby is asleep to do my work, and he wakes up late. And I go off to sleep by 10 p.m. after feeding the baby and putting her to sleep. And he stays up till about 3 a.m. to do his work. This is the only way we can reserve energy for a kid during daytime.

—**TANYA M.,** mother of one, USA

Start your day with a D3 review

Every day when I look at my to-do list, both work and home, it seems overwhelming. The first thing I do is give it the D3 review. Which of these items can be: (1) Delayed; (2) Delegated to another member of your team (it is not dumping on them, it is an opportunity for them to learn new skills); (3) Doesn't need to get done! Paring down what "has to be done today" reduces my stress!

—**LORI K.,** mother of two, USA

Borrow from agile

We have a Kanban board (software development version) for household chores. To-Do—Doing—Done. The kids (as most of us) prefer a pulling system rather than a pushing one. It gave them a feeling of independence in terms of what and when to do their parts. It led to less nagging and as a parent, I became more a coach than a boss. The system developed over time, with chores becoming more equally sized in terms of time (and tediousness), rules like "you can't take the same chore two times in a row," and due dates.

—**MAGNUS A.,** father of four, Sweden

Find the teaching opportunities

We established the "International Corona School" and the "students" would get stars for doing things and doing them right. The tasks included taking care of the cat, setting the table, taking out the garbage, hanging the clothes . . . and the total number of stars achieved on a given day would double if these things were done "over and above" or without being asked. We included "extracurriculars" such as cooking classes, or experiments such as observing how mold grew differently on slices of toasted bread after we touched them with washed hands and unwashed hands. I wore a ribbon in my hair and the kids called me "Frau Bego" to symbolically separate schooltime from the rest of the day.

—**BEGOÑA S.,** mother of three and stepmother of two, Austria

Grandparents make great teachers

I asked the grandparents to get involved with the homeschooling during lockdown (by Skype, so socially distanced). The kids and grandparents both loved this idea, and they all prepared for it and looked forward to it every week. They taught about curriculum-related history topics but in greater depth than expected at school and introduced the kids to two foreign languages! Better than if we'd homeschooled alone, and it meant my husband and I could get more work done.

—**SALLY H.,** mother of two, UK

Outsource, be honest, and let go of perfection

I am a single mom by choice with a toddler. While the current crisis was beyond my imagination, I did put quite a bit of thought and planning into building a sustainable, enjoyable life for us. Here's what helps me get through:

- Outsource what you can afford to outsource. If you have the resources, hire someone to deep clean your home once a month, pay the extra to have groceries and other essentials delivered (and tip really well for the privilege), and budget for childcare. Some of that went out the window with the pandemic, but knowing the limits of what you can accomplish is key.

- Be honest and up front with colleagues. I cannot ever join a call during dinner or bedtime. And, I can't always dial in to an unplanned call outside of my normal hours either. It's OK to set boundaries.

- Let go. The house isn't pristine, the grass needs to get cut, and I order takeout once or twice a week. It's not perfect but it's good enough.

—**VICTORIA T.,** mother of one, USA

Nap time is focus time

If your child still takes regular naps, block your calendar for the duration of the nap: no Zoom or phone calls. Set aside this time to either focus on tasks that require your full attention or have a quick coffee break or alone time to recharge.

—**LILLA N.,** mother of two, the Netherlands

Make time to connect with your partner

Open communication matters. Talk openly about what your expectations are; be realistic.

Communicate with your spouse about what your priorities are and how to divide household responsibilities. Delegate what you can. Outsource what you can. Let the rest go.

Supporting each other goes beyond the to-do list. It is also about being present for each other. Proactively create a plan together for how you and your spouse will connect with each other: whether it's 15 minutes midday between Zoom calls or after kiddo bedtime. Make a point to ask about your spouse's stories or worries from work. The more you can connect and help each other feel heard on the big things, the less the little things will matter.

—**SHANNA H.,** mother of one, USA

Show each other your work

The crisis is bringing our families together in new ways through the remote work, education, and play, all done from our homes. For instance, in the past I would go to my industry trade shows and conferences without my family, leaving home on Sunday night and not seeing them for a week. Today I connect to the events remotely from home, with my family "joining me" for selected public parts like spectacular industry shows and keynotes with celebrities.
—**PETER K.,** father of three, USA

Chores for all, respect space, practice gratitude

Some things I've learnt as we have huddled together over this period:

- A preset, intentional mealtime is a good and needed rest from work. Have a menu planned that the family looks forward to and leave the phone face down.

- Create chores for all to take part in, no matter how young or old. We each call this place home and it is a great way to increase the sense of family.

- Give everyone a space that others learn to respect. Knock and wait for a reply before entering!

121

- Practice intentional gratitude—it is a great time to learn to have a positive attitude, regardless.

—**PRAISE M.,** mother of four, Singapore

Let go of screen guilt

Honestly, giving ourselves permission to use media (learnings apps, Netflix, and YouTube principally) was simply a necessity. We finally lifted the guilt associated with screen time. And thinking long term, the increase in quality family time in comparison to the increased screen time, I evaluate as a net positive for the family.

—**ADAM H.,** father of three, USA

Work late, carve dedicated time, smile through the chaos

I certainly won't win mom of the year for these tips, but they've kept me sane to date:

- Taking on a few late-night (or all-night) work sessions to play catch up. I'm a firm believer in getting enough sleep, but sometimes having made a dent in my work to-do list really helps me cope mentally with the juggling in the day (more than a decent night's sleep would have).

- Carving out dedicated time. So much of my day is spent multitasking, and I realised pretty quickly that letting my daughter colour in my office while I finish up a deadline or my baby crawls around my feet while on a conference call, doesn't count. So, even if it's 30 minutes to share lunch, play and laugh and be present.

- As someone who normally sweats the small stuff, I'm trying not to take the late submissions, kitchen messes, or bad days too seriously. I don't want to look back on this time with regrets for how I showed up for my family each day. I want to remember how happy we all were, cooped up in our home, in amongst the chaos.

—**NICOLA B.,** mother of two, South Africa

Step back if you need to

My husband travels regularly for his job as an insurance adjuster and has been out of town for most of the shutdown. I tried to balance it all by myself, but it was too much—I felt like I was going to have a stroke and the kids were miserable. I saw a social media post from a teacher advising not to worry about the kids falling behind academically—they're trained and ready to fix that later; it's the emotional trauma that can't be repaired and can lead to so many other lifelong problems. That influenced me enough to take family medical leave until school or childcare resume. From that point on I threw myself into their nontraditional instruction and made sure that another sunny day didn't pass us by.

—**ERIN K.,** mother of two, USA

Set boundaries, for your children and yourself

We've had to develop some new boundaries for us all to thrive.

"Stoplight" boundaries for my teens:

- Red light: Don't bug me right now unless someone is bleeding or something is on fire.

- Yellow light: It's OK to interrupt me briefly if there's something that seems urgent.

- Green light: Come on in if you like—I'm not in a meeting, but bring some homework or a book so that we can work quietly together.

Boundaries for me:

- Set clear "at work" hours and keep them.

- Make it clear to my family when I'm off the clock. This includes staying out of my home office as much as possible outside of working hours.

- When a critical deadline or short-fuse project calls for a few extra work hours, I need to own this, be transparent with my family about the departure from the norm, and apologize. I need to be sure my kiddos know I'm not choosing work over them when I'm supposed to "at home."

- Step outside and get at least a little natural light every day.

—**QUINN B.**, father of six, USA

Don't go it alone

Grow your "extended family." It's so easy to set up a group on WhatsApp or Telegram where fellow parents can share their tips and crowdsource solutions that are relevant to your context. Don't fall for the idea that you have to wing it alone; there are so many parents in the same shoes as you.

—**OSEMHEN O.**, mother of two, Nigeria

You can't do it all after bedtime

I can caution against my poor strategy of relying too much on doing everything after my toddler's bedtime when productivity feels highest. Good strategies include using a robot vacuum cleaner.

—**LINDA L.**, mother of one, Sweden

Help your grown kids

As a grandparent, our children are working and trying to balance work and home with their children 24-7. They are managing despite lots of stresses. However, we older parents need to be sensitive to their needs (they're always our children, that never ends). We need to kick in and help them too if we live close enough or maybe travel to help. Ask them, "Can I take the kids for the weekend?" to give them a break. Give them some alone time, make them recharge! It's a way to help our children and show them our love for family. Don't wait for them to ask but be proactive and ask them. They will appreciate it.

—**ROB P.,** father of two and grandfather of two, USA

Take the long view

My stress went down when I realized that looking back at this time in 20 years, the situation will be for my kid "that cool year I had a six-month holiday." After all, plenty of people take a sabbatical or a gap year . . . it's a unique experience for her.

—**PATRICE O.,** father of one, Canada

Adapted from "HBR Readers on Juggling Work and Kids . . . in a Pandemic," on hbr.org, July 22, 2020 (product #H05QTZ).

15

How Working Parents Can Manage the Demands of School-Age Kids

by Daisy Dowling

Quick Takes

- Explain your reasons when you have to leave work
- Plan and bundle volunteer commitments
- Invest in the educational activities that matter most
- Try a "family study hall"
- Treat teachers as valued colleagues

Your task list is endless, your stress level high. And a lot of the work and worry seems to be coming from one place: your child's school.

As a working parent, you've already got two jobs—and having two jobs isn't easy. But you're also going to spend a minimum of 13 years with a third critical role: stewarding your child's education. It's a position that comes with enormous hope and pressure. You want the absolute best for your children, and you're determined to oversee their school experience in a way that will set them up for success in college and life beyond. But it's a position that can create significant practical challenges for any family.

But here's the good news: There *are* effective ways to manage the overwhelming demands of drop-off, homework, and parent-teacher conferences while still delivering and succeeding at work.

Here, gleaned from teachers, school administrators, and experienced parents themselves, are a few of the simple, specific techniques that put any working parent of school-age kids on their front foot—and they'll work for your family, too.

Explain the *why*, not just the *when*, of time away from work

Instead of telling your boss and colleagues that you'll be "out of the office tomorrow afternoon," explain that "I'll be leaving the office tomorrow afternoon for two hours for a parent-teacher meeting at Brandon's school. We've been concerned about his math scores, and we're talking with the teacher about how to support him over the summer and into next year. I'll be back online by 6 p.m., and we can go over the budget draft at tomorrow's meeting." The second statement makes it vastly easier for colleagues to understand, sympathize, and ally themselves with you—and does a better job of telegraphing your commitment to the job as well.

Plan and bundle volunteer commitments

Even with a very flexible job, it's unlikely that any working parent can make it to every bake sale, library fundraiser, and field trip. Here's what you do: In the first week of school, tell your child's teachers and/or the school's volunteer coordinators that you're eager to do your fair share—but that you will be doing it all in one go. You'll schedule a personal or vacation day well in advance and use it entirely for school volunteerism. Maybe you'll be the "reading helper" in your daughter's second-grade class in the morning, walk the school's neighborhood safety patrol in the afternoon, and take the minutes during the PTA fundraising committee meeting at 5 p.m. When the day is over, enjoy knowing that your yearly contribution has been made in full—and efficiently.

Invest your time where it matters most

All working parents have packed schedules, yet "in our desire to fully engage with our children's education, many of us gravitate to time-intensive activities that may not actually have much impact on their success in school," says Ariela Rozman, a leading K-12 education expert and founding partner of EdNavigator, a not-for-profit that provides custom coaching and tools for parents seeking to keep their children on track in school. Rozman adds: "There may be great reasons for you to take part in school fundraising, attend school events, or help your child with their homework each evening. Maybe you want to support the school community or simply to spend time together with your kid. But think about putting some time toward the things that are proven to produce great results too." Rozman cites "The Broken Compass," a groundbreaking and comprehensive research study done by professors from the University of Texas and Duke University.[1] They found that a handful of habits make a real difference, such as reading aloud to young kids and talking to teenagers about college plans.

Make "family study hall" a habit

Beat the nightly homework drama (the nagging, the power struggles, the bargaining, the tears) by setting a hard-and-fast time each evening that the whole family has study hall: silent, dedicated work time around the dining table. The kids do their homework, and you catch up on office emails or reading. When the kitchen timer rings, study hall is over, and the whole family gets to enjoy downtime or a relaxing activity like watching a favorite TV program together. This routine may not be easy for the first few nights you try it, but the kids will quickly adjust, and the benefits are many. They will learn how to focus better, to work more efficiently, and to use the "sprint and recover" approach when tackling a large workload—all skills that will make them more successful and happier in school and in their futures. You'll also have established a clear boundary between work and play—something that's vital and healthy for the entire family in our always-on world.

Treat teachers and administrators as you would valued colleagues (because that's what they are)

For many parents, the parent-teacher relationship is fraught and unclear: Is the teacher an all-powerful evaluator, capable of changing your child's future with a few strokes of a red pen? Or a vendor who needs to be constantly nudged if you're going to get decent service? Will there be terrible consequences for your child if you dial into a parent-teacher meeting while on a business trip? The answer to all of those is no—but you *do* need to develop strong working relationships with the professionals teaching your child. To do so, think of a favorite coworker, one you enjoy being staffed with on tough projects. The coworker is someone you constantly communicate with, sharing all critical information; someone you greet setbacks and roadblocks with by saying, "Let's figure out how to solve this together"; someone whose constructive comments you take graciously, offering your own in a spirit of respect, trust, and good humor. Take this exact same approach with educators: Tell Mrs. Wilson that you'll be away on business next week, in case your third-grader acts out; flag it when Susie is struggling with her Spanish homework—and ask what the best way is to support her; let the science teacher know your son loved the chemistry experiment. Teachers are professionals—and humans. They'll notice and appreciate your collaboration, and likely respond in kind.

Remember what you're managing toward

School, with all of its deadlines, complexity, evaluations, and social pressures, can be a daunting experience, for kids and for their parents. Amid all the noise and busy-ness, it can be helpful to recenter by remembering the two key outcomes you—and every parent—are really shooting for: *independence* and *opportunity*. You want your son or daughter to develop into a competent, re-sponsible adult capable of managing in a complex world. And you want them to find the maximum possible num-ber of open doors in terms of college and, later, in terms of career. But you don't need to ensure your child has a flawless, completely bump-and-bruise-free experience at school in order to get there. It's OK—desirable, even—for your child to struggle with long division or have an argu-ment on the playground, or for you to miss a few soccer games. These things may be upsetting in the moment, particularly to you as a high-achieving professional, but they're the experiences your child needs to become re-silient, independent, and ultimately successful in their own right.

Parenting school-age children while making it happen in a full-time career can feel like an uphill marathon of a task—long, constant, and steep. But remember: School won't be the only place your child gets their education. Like all parents, you will teach your child the greatest lessons: the importance of hard work, the value of com-mitments to family, and the satisfaction that comes from a tough job well done.

Adapted from content posted on hbr.org, June 13, 2018 (product #H04DW0).

16

Stop Feeling Guilty About Your To-Do List

by Rebecca Knight

Quick Takes

- Recognize that supporting others *is* being productive
- Accept that your to-do list will never be done
- Trim down your list and make the goals credibly achievable
- Let go of goals that aren't worth your investment
- Be prepared to work through your emotions again and again

You're getting that feeling again: You've been busy for hours, and your to-do list has barely been touched. You feel guilty for not getting more done. But this emotion is neither useful nor healthy. So, what can you do about it? How should you handle feelings that you're letting down your coworkers, boss, kids—and even yourself? How can you learn to accept that you are doing the best you can? And, what are some strategies for getting smarter about how you tackle your interminable to-do list?

What the Experts Say

Your end-of-the-day shame for not having accomplished what you set out to is often the result of unrealistic expectations, says Heidi Grant, the director of research and development for Americas Learning at EY and the author of *Nine Things Successful People Do Differently*, among others. "Most humans are overly optimistic—we enter the day with an expectation and plan of getting all sorts of things done," she says. But the trouble is, "we are not grounding our expectations in the reality of the work that we do."

So invariably by the end of the day, we feel anxious and guilt-ridden, says Whitney Johnson, executive coach and author of *Disrupt Yourself*. "You look at what you didn't get done, and you get that sinking feeling deep in your soul that you are not enough." But, she says, "you mustn't feel like a failure." Conquering this guilt involves a combination of getting savvier about how you chip away at your to-do list, improving how you manage your own (and others') expectations about what you can realistically achieve over the course of a day, and building self-compassion for those times when you fail to live up to them. Here's how.

Reframe the situation

When the nagging voice in your head tells you that you're failing those around you with your inability to finish certain tasks, Grant says you need to recognize those negative ruminations for what they are, "a story you're telling yourself." After all, "it's not objectively true that you should feel bad about this or that; it's only true because of the way you're interpreting the situation," she says. "You're deciding that it's all your fault." Instead, seize the opportunity to reframe and reappraise the situation. "Ask yourself: Is there another way to look at this?" You might, for instance, come to realize that "I did a lot today, and I did my best. I hope to get more done tomorrow, and my colleagues and family probably understand because they're busy, too."

Gain perspective on your productivity

It's also helpful to think about the factors that keep you from accomplishing items on your list and appreciating that, oftentimes, circumstances cannot be helped. "When you think about why you aren't getting things done, more often than not it's because you were attending to someone else's needs," says Johnson. "Your client, colleague, boss, or family member needed your help, and you provided it." Johnson recommends replacing the question, *What did I accomplish today?* with *How did I contribute today?* "You will find you were more productive than you thought."

Recognize your limitations

Some work-related guilt involves feelings of shame about your inability to reach your full potential—as in, "If I worked harder and longer, I'd achieve more," says Grant. This anxiety may be due, in part, to "the myths of growth mindset." Today's workplace indoctrinates employees into thinking they can always get better at something—so long as they put in the effort. But while "improvement is always possible, you also need the goal to improve"—not to mention the time, energy, and resources to do so. So, when you find yourself feeling guilty because you're not succeeding in the way you envisioned, try to recognize that this emotion stems "from not wanting to reckon with your limitations," she says. You need to "disengage from the things that are less important to you," she adds. "Never give up something because you think you can't do it; give up because you've decided it's not worth investing your time and energy." Put simply, "Pick your battles and let the rest of it go."

Get pragmatic about your to-do list

In addition to dealing with the psychological effects of falling short on your to-do list, there are plenty of ways you can get better at allocating your time—which could also help reduce your end-of-the-day shame. It starts with taming your list.

- **Perform a forensic analysis.** Grant recommends trying an experiment. Each morning, write a regular to-do list, and at the end of the day, see how many things you managed to complete. Do this for a week or two. "Then ask, on average, how many items am I crossing off?" Your goal is to get a feel for how much work you actually get done in a day, so you can learn to manage your expectations about what's realistic.

- **Pare down your list.** Then you need to "right-size your list," says Johnson. It's demoralizing when, at the end of the day, your to-do list with 20 items has only one or two crossed off. No wonder you feel guilty. "Lengthy lists are unrealistic," she says. Trim it down, and make the goals on it credibly achievable.

- **Be deliberate about where you focus.** "The key to not feeling guilty at the end of the day depends on how you tackle the beginning of your day," says Johnson. "As you're writing your to-do list, select a few things you really need to get done and concentrate on those." Be ruthless about how you prioritize your time. "There are only so many hours in the day, and you have to make choices about where to focus," says Grant.

- **Pay attention to how your list evolves—or doesn't.** If you notice certain items tend to linger on your list, Grant suggests asking yourself: What is the difference between what I am crossing off and what remains? Is it because I don't know where to start? Is it because the tasks are too high level? Do they need to be broken up into smaller chunks? Or am I missing opportunities to chip away at these tasks? "It may be an indication that you need to book time in your calendar to do them because you're not going to do them spontaneously."

- **Embrace the state of noncompletion.** Try to cultivate a degree of comfort with the notion that "you will never be caught up, and you will always have things at the end of the day that you really wished you'd gotten to," says Grant. "Make peace with it," she says. Accept the fact that your to-do list will be in a constant "state of noncompletion," she adds. This is particularly true at work once you reach a certain level in the hierarchy of your organization. "If you can embrace it, it starts to hurt less."

Set expectations

Once you've developed an understanding of your bandwidth and retooled your to-do list accordingly, it's time to set expectations with others at work. "Avoid people pleasing," and "stop overpromising," says Johnson. Being explicit about what's reasonable for you to take on "prevents constant requests coming in for things you can't do," adds Grant. "It also helps establish boundaries for you, which is reaffirming." What's more, being clear about what you can manage often helps you recognize that in general, your colleagues and boss are understanding and reasonable people (see chapter 11, "How to Say No to Taking on More"). "We tend to imagine people having far worse reactions than they actually do. When you inform people of your constraints and they take it in stride, which they usually will, you realize there is nothing to feel bad about," she says.

Practice self-empathy

Sure, you can be a little shrewder about how you manage your time, and you can set better expectations, but in the end, "you have to be a steward of your own well-being," says Grant. You need to figure out a way to "preserve your mental capacity" and "stop obsessing about your to-do list." You can only do "one thing at a time, and that's never going to change." Instead of fixating on three things you didn't finish, pat yourself on the back for the 17 things you did, adds Johnson. Positive self-talk comes in handy here, too. Try a new mantra. "Tell yourself, 'I worked hard today; I gave it my best shot; I did a good job, and I should be proud of that.'"

Be patient

Similarly, don't expect a fast and simple solution to the problem. "You're not going to read this article and never experience guilt again," says Grant. Grappling with guilt is ongoing. "Expect to have feelings of guilt and have to work through them again and again," she says. Johnson concurs. "Sometimes you will struggle with this more, sometimes less," she says. "It's a process." Thankfully, if you implement these practices—in particular, accepting a certain degree of noncompletion—"it will get easier."

Adapted from content posted on hbr.org, March 9, 2020 (product #H05GWB).

You Can't Be in Two Places at Once

Deal with Tough Work-Family Conflicts

17

Winning Support for Flexible Work

by Amy Gallo

Quick Takes

- Ask yourself what you want to accomplish

- Propose it as an experiment

- Consult with your team

- Highlight the benefits to your company

M any working parents seek flexible work arrangements to accommodate lives that don't mesh with being present in an office on a traditional schedule, five days a week. And research from Lotte Bailyn, MIT management professor and coauthor of *Beyond Work-Family Balance*, shows that when employees have the flexibility they need, they meet goals more easily, they're absent or tardy less often, and their morale goes up. Yet not every company has an official policy or program for alternative arrangements—and not every manager is willing or equipped to provide them for members of their teams. This doesn't mean you should give up on the idea of flextime if it would help you feel less harried, cut down a lengthy commute, be more present with your kids, or avoid burnout. It just means that the onus is on you to propose a plan that works for you, your boss, and your company. By focusing your proposal on the benefits research has shown and thoughtfully framing your request around them, you greatly increase your chances of getting approval for an alternative work arrangement.

Define What You Want

The first step is to figure out what you're trying to accomplish. Is your goal to spend more time with family? Less time at the office? Or do you want to remove distractions so you can focus on bigger, longer-term projects? Once you're clear on your goal, decide how you can achieve it while still doing your job effectively. Options include a compressed workweek, a job share, working remotely, and taking a sabbatical. Of course, not every job is suited to a flexible arrangement. Before you make a proposal, think about the impact your wished-for scenario will have on your boss, your team, and your performance.

Next, investigate what policies, if any, your company has and whether there's a precedent for flexibility. You won't need to blaze a trail if one already exists.

Design It as an Experiment

Some managers will hesitate to approve a flexible work arrangement, especially if your organization lacks established protocols. Allay their fears by positioning your proposal as an experiment. "Include a trial period so your boss doesn't worry that things will fall apart," says Bailyn. "He or she needs to be able to see the new way of working."

In his book *Total Leadership: Be a Better Leader, Have a Richer Life*, Stewart D. Friedman talks about nine types of experiments you can do to gently introduce flexibility—everything from working remotely to delegating. Whatever you propose, provide an out. Explain that if it doesn't work, you're willing to try a different arrangement or resume your former routine. "One can always go back to the original plan, but most such experiments work out very well," says Bailyn.

Ask for Team Input

"Our research has shown that flexibility only works when it's done collectively, not one-on-one between employee and employer," says Bailyn. Your team is affected by your work schedule, so you need everyone's support to make your new arrangement a success. Explain what you're trying to achieve, and ask for their input. "Engage them in the planning," Bailyn says, and let your boss know that you've incorporated your colleagues' suggestions into your proposal.

Involving your team can help head off another common concern: Some bosses worry that if they grant one person flexibility, the floodgates will open and everyone will want the same arrangement. This is often an unfounded fear. Friedman points out that there's a difference between *equality* and *equity*, and, in fact, many people prefer a traditional schedule. "You don't give everyone the same thing because they don't *want* the same thing," he says.

Highlight the Benefits to the Organization

Emphasize the organizational benefits over the personal ones. "Whatever you try has to be designed very consciously to not just be about you or your family," Friedman says. "Instead, have the clear goal of improving your performance at work and making your boss successful." Demonstrate that you have considered the company's needs, that your new arrangement will not be disruptive, and that it will actually have positive benefits, such as improving your productivity or increasing your relevant knowledge.

Reassess and Make Adjustments

Once your flexible work arrangement has been in place for three or four months, evaluate its success. Are you reaching your goals? Is the arrangement causing problems for anyone? Because you've designed it as a trial, you'll want to report back to your boss. "Get the data to support your productivity. Show that it's working," says Friedman. And if it's not, be prepared to suggest changes.

Adapted from content posted on hbr.org, December 1, 2010 (product #H006JJ).

18

How to Handle Work When Your Child Is Sick

by Daisy Dowling

Quick Takes

- Have a backup plan
- Communicate your sick plan to your team ahead of time
- Make your pediatrician your ally
- Explore alternatives to doctor's office visits
- Be willing to break your usual rules with your kids

Mommy/Daddy, I don't feel so good.

It's a phrase that, along with its nonverbal equivalent—that glazed, pale, listless look that your kids get when they're coming down with something—that you've learned to dread. Because whatever the ailment, be it flu, stomach bug, sprain, or other, two things are now certain: (1) You're going to spend the next 24 hours, and likely more, worrying about and helping your child to get better, wishing you could magically take their discomfort away; and (2) You're simultaneously going to spend all of that time in a frantic, improvisational rush trying to cover responsibilities at work while taking care of business at home—which won't, to put it mildly, be easy.

While there's no silver bullet, the good news is that with a few specific strategies for managing your colleagues, care arrangement, and, yes, yourself, you can mitigate the situation and make it through these roughest patches of working parenthood in one physical, emotional, and professional piece.

Acknowledge and anticipate

Because working parenthood is so demanding on a daily basis, it's natural to want to avoid thinking about the times it will actually become harder. But acknowledging that you and your child are both human, and therefore will become ill, is the critical first step to avoiding crises and undue stress. According to the National Institutes of Health, small children routinely get 8 to 10 colds and viruses per year, or nearly one per month. Accept the inevitable, and anticipate how you will handle it logistically: Call in Grandma—or the backup babysitter? Take turns with your partner covering at home? Telecommute? Cancel the monthly sales trip? The more specific and feasible the plan you develop, the less daunting the situation will seem when it comes.

Communicate ahead of time

Tell your boss and key colleagues the game plan if your child gets sick. Alert them straight-up as to the flexibility you require—but in a way that underscores your dedication: "Jordan normally goes to daycare from 8 a.m. to 5 p.m. If he gets sick and needs to stay home, my mother-in-law should be able to cover until 3 p.m. I'll then need to head home and will work remotely for the rest of the afternoon. If anything urgent comes up while I'm out of the office, please never hesitate to reach out."

Control the controllables

Minimize last-minute tasks and logistical headaches by "playing through" your backup plan. If you'll be dropping a sick child at Aunt Susan's house, make sure that Aunt Susan always has Children's Tylenol, knows when she's allowed to give it, and how much. If working from home is the strategy, ensure that your remote log-in system not only allows you access to documents but also permits you to print them. Always keep a "sick-child go bag"—stocked with basic medicines, change of comfy clothes, healthy snacks, books/toys/stuffed animal, and other key supplies—inside the front-hall closet, ready to be thrown into the car. Put key resources in place ahead of when you need them, and you'll avoid undue emergency.

Find—and budget in—the resources

Most working parents are on a tight financial regiment: The cost of childcare alone is enough to strain even a high-earning household's budget, and that's before even factoring in food, clothing, or college savings. But to the practical and financial extent possible, try to find the extra resources that will help sustain your family and performance when your child is ill. It could be paying for delivery from the 24-hour pharmacy, taking an Uber instead of the train to work so you're not late coming straight from the pediatrician's, or occasionally getting professional in-home backup care from a local service. These things are expensive—frustratingly so—but they're investments in your ability to perform on the job while taking good care of your family. Identify the ones most useful to you and allocate what you can into an annual "working parent emergency fund" that you can draw on as needed.

Make your pediatrician an ally

You've made certain that your child has a warm, competent, and trustworthy medical caregiver. But as a working parent, it also helps if that caregiver has early-morning, after-work, and/or weekend office hours; has a decent wireless network in the waiting room; and keeps your payment information on file so that you can avoid time-delaying paperwork when the appointment is over. Check if there are speakerphones in the exam rooms, or ask the staff if they're willing to FaceTime or Skype an appointment—that way, if you're traveling for work when your child sprains her wrist and has to make a sudden visit to the doctor, you can be as present as possible. Remember: The doctor and office staff are probably working parents, too.

Be willing to break all your (usual) rules

As a committed, on-the-job parent, you've got standards around screen time, healthy eating, and sleep habits, just to name a few. But when your kid is sick and home with a backup caregiver, it's not the time to keep the iPad and cookie jar on lockdown. When facing constraints in one area, be willing to relax standards in others. When everyone's well, you'll quickly get back into regular routine.

Stay connected—but not on social media

For most of us, using Facebook, Twitter, and other social media services has become as natural as breathing. But if your manager and colleagues have been supportive of your working from home while the baby's sick, nothing will erode their goodwill and generosity faster than seeing you posting new pictures on Facebook. If you're out of the office because your child is unwell, focus on keeping strong and regular lines of communication with colleagues—be as responsive as possible on email, call to check in—but keep that communication through professional channels.

If the problem is longer-term, engage with your organization—not just your manager—for support

As stressful as it is to have a child home with the flu while you're facing a huge marketing deadline, it's a short-term situation; in a week, it will pass. But if the challenge isn't a short-term one—if you've learned that your child has a chronic or acute health issue, for example—alert your organization immediately. Unless senior managers and HR know what's happening, they can't extend deadlines, find you additional resources, help you set up a leave of absence, alert the insurance company of needed care, or refer you to Alan in the Chicago office—whose child recently went through the same thing.

Don't make it your child's problem

Whatever your child's ailment, they feel crummy already. It won't help the situation any, and will only make them feel worse, to witness your frustration and stress. When your toddler spikes a fever the night before the corporate tax filing is due, don't react with an "oh no!" and hand-wringing—simply reassure her that Mommy or Daddy will make certain she feels better soon.

Remember why you're working in the first place: to provide for your family, keep a safe and stable home, and earn toward your child's education. While missing a key meeting or leaving a sick child at home while you head out to the office will feel lousy in the moment, remind yourself that you're managing toward what matters in the long run—and that you're doing the best you can.

Adapted from content posted on hbr.org, June 18, 2017 (product #H03S47).

19

What to Do When Personal and Professional Commitments Compete for Your Time

by Elizabeth Grace Saunders

Quick Takes

- Reflect on how you're going to deal with conflicts before they come up

- Avoid defaulting to an "all-or-nothing" approach

- Consider delegating, time-splitting, or virtual presence

- Show your commitment or care in other ways when you just can't be there

Y ou're double-booked.

It's not just one meeting scheduled over another. It's something for your family at odds with a work commitment. These situations can trigger guilt and stress. Guilt because you feel like you're letting others down—no matter what you decide, you will lose. And stress because you literally can't be in two places at once.

As a time-management coach, I help working parents navigate these challenges on a daily basis. I've found that there are two different components that you must address to minimize both guilt and stress.

The first is to define how you want to prioritize your time when professional and personal commitments collide. Each person must determine this prioritization for themselves because dramatic differences exist between individuals' preferences, especially across cultures.

Block out time on your calendar to think about what seems right for you and your family. That way you've done some thoughtful reflection in advance of a potentially intense decision. As you think about your general guidelines for when to choose for work versus family commitments, explore these facets:

- **Values.** To feel successful, you need to live according to your values. Ask yourself: What are my values in terms of the type of spouse, parent, and employee I want to be? What choices will I be happy that I made five years from now?

- **Family culture.** Every family has a different flavor in terms of what matters to them. Ask yourself: What kind of family culture do I want to create? Do I value eating meals together, going to kids' activities, or spending quality time with my spouse? What decisions would be aligned with that culture?

- **Individual preferences.** To some children, having you show up at certain events may be a big deal whereas to others, it's not. Ask them when it's most important to them that you show up. The same is true with your spouse. Find out what they need to feel supported and connected with you. The key question is: What matters most to the people in my family?

- **Job constraints.** Certain positions require more travel or more work outside of normal business hours. Ask yourself: What's truly required? Where do I have flexibility?

Once you've determined a general working model for how you want to make decisions, you can make choices with less guilt. Your sense of "rightness" will be determined by being congruent with your internal values system, not with how other people react to you for working or spending time with family.

After you've thought through an overall strategy for how you want to address work and family time conflicts, expand your thinking on the number of options available to you in situations where you wish you could bilocate but can't.

Some people revert too quickly to an all-or-nothing approach, meaning they're completely engaged in one commitment and disengaged in another. But from my vantage point, there are at least four other potential options to consider:

- **Delegate.** Although you can't be two places at once, someone else may be able to go in your place. At work, perhaps another colleague could represent your department at a meeting or event. At home, you could potentially work out a carpool situation with a neighbor if after-school pickup is an issue.

- **Time split.** Sometimes you can get most of the value even if you show up for just part of the time. For example, you could attend the meet-and-greet portion of a professional event but leave before dinner so you can still see most of your son's game.

- **Virtual presence.** Being virtually present at key times can make a huge difference in how supported people feel. For instance, maybe you attend your son's speech tournament, but you call in to meetings that happen when your son isn't competing. Or perhaps you must be at a sales meeting, but you call your daughter before her gymnastics meet to see how she's doing, get updates via text throughout, and call after to let her talk through how she feels about how it went.

- **Invest in advance.** Finally, for the times that you really do need to be all-in for work or all-in for family commitments, you can still find a way to have a presence with some forethought. When you must miss an important work meeting, look over the agenda in advance and email your thoughts to demonstrate that you want to make a contribution to the discussion. And if you can't go to your son's or daughter's actual show, go see the dress rehearsal. Putting in effort to be present in advance makes a statement that you care.

No matter how well you plan, times will come up where work and family commitments come head-to-head. These situations rarely feel easy. But with some reflection, you can reduce the guilt around your decisions and decrease stress by finding ways to make your presence and support felt in both worlds, even when you can't literally be in two places at once.

Adapted from content posted on hbr.org, April 26, 2018 (product #H04ASY).

20

Keep Your Home Life Sane When Work Gets Crazy

by Stewart D. Friedman

Quick Takes

- Accept that the many aspects of your life will not always be in equilibrium

- Discuss work-family conflicts with your family when they arise

- Learn what they really need and expect from you

- Keep the conversation open when your workload returns to normal

When you're going through a phase that compels you to put more time, effort, brainpower, and heart into your job, how do you work it out with your family and others who matter in your life? And how do you make sure this spike in your focus on work doesn't become a "new normal" that extends indefinitely into the future? The short answer: Dialogue about what matters most—to you and to them.

First, forget *balance*, which is a misguided metaphor for what success looks like in the different parts of life. It's not possible to have perfect equilibrium among the four domains of life—work, home, community, and self—every day, every week, or even every year. Naturally, there are times when any one of these aspects of your life has to take center stage.

When a spike in work-related activities is having a deleterious effect on your family or on some other part of your life, then it's time for what I call *stakeholder dialogues*—conversations with the people who matter most about your mutual expectations and how best to meet them, now and in the long run.

Here are five steps to take in such conversations:

1. **Provide context** by letting people at home (or in your community) know why your work temporarily demands your attention to an extraordinary degree. As in, "Let me give you a bit of background about what's happening . . . " Keep it short. This is not an excuse, just a brief explanation to set the stage for dialogue.

2. **Explain the purpose** of what you're doing at work and why you believe it's important, not solely for your own growth but for the positive impact you hope to have on others. As in, "By my devoting this effort now I'll be able to ____, which is important to us because it'll help us to ____."

3. **Ask about the consequences** they believe will result from this shift in your attention toward work. Learn more about what this adjustment means for them. As in, "Can you tell me how this will make things harder for you?" and then follow up with "Can you give me an example?" Do not try to minimize the difficulties they report; instead, compassionately inquire.

4. **Express genuine remorse** for disappointments or hurt you might be causing, being specific about your understanding of how your actions

are creating stresses and strains. As in "I'm sorry that my being unavailable is hurting you." Own it.

5. **Explore possible alternatives** for how you might minimize these negative effects. As in, "I'm not sure what might help, but do you have ideas for what I can do to try to make this better for us, our family, our relationship?" And ask again: "What other thoughts do you have about what I can do, either now or sometime in the future?"

You're likely to discover possibilities for actions you can take that won't cost you much but will help to minimize any damage caused by your work spike. You might even improve the quality of your relationships with your family, friends, and others in your life.

Assuming that if you're not home for dinner, your family is losing out, or you're losing out, may not be an accurate read. Maybe driving your daughter to school is more important to her than your being home for dinner. Your spouse might be happy to meet you in town for dinner, even if you have to return to the office while they head home afterward. Maybe they don't care so much if your travel increases or the length of your workday increases, as long as they have your *undivided* attention when you are at home. You won't know until you ask (see chapter 8, "How to Spend Your Parenting Time and Energy Wisely").

What I've found is that what others expect of you is usually a bit less than, and somewhat different from, what you think they expect of you. And unless you know what's essential and meaningful to them, now and in the future, you can't generate creative solutions that make sense for all of you.

Once you've navigated your way through an especially tumultuous episode at work and managed to keep your domestic ship of state on course, it's useful to be deliberate again in choosing a path forward that suits all parties. You might want to mark the end of that period as a special occasion with a celebratory dinner, as a way of closing the book on it.

Then, keep your stakeholder dialogues going as you return to a normal workload. Take a bit of time to review which of the strategies you employed worked well and which did not. The key is remaining open to discovering new ways of adjusting—either at work or at home—that let you pursue what you care about most, no matter what the world throws at you.

Adapted from content posted on hbr.org, February 23, 2015 (product #H01W2T).

21

Managing Work During a Family Crisis

by Sabina Nawaz

Quick Takes

- Manage the flow of information
- Clarify your preferences and expectations
- Take care of yourself every day
- Find strength in numbers

had two conversations in the same week. One with the minister and my parents on how to conduct my mother's impending memorial service. The other was a meeting with my son and his psychiatrist about how to have a plan for when he is suicidal," said Rhonda, a senior manager and thought leader in her field.

One day amid a flourishing career, you might find your personal life in crisis and threatening to upend your professional life. If so, you're not alone.

"When you're successful like I've been in my career, you pick positive adjectives for yourself. You don't use the word 'alcoholic.'" With two young kids and a wife, Derek, an executive at a global firm, felt defeated for the first time.

Just before boarding a flight from Boston to London to meet with a major client, Anique received a call from her 10-year-old daughter Jasmine, not to wish her bon voyage but in the throes of a panic attack. This initiated an 18-month journey through Jasmine's struggles with acute anxiety.

These are stories related by successful executives among my coaching clients who have faced family crises jeopardizing their performance at work. Some have struggled with a snowballing challenge for years, afraid to admit the problem and seek help. For others, the downward spiral was precipitated by a routine trip to the doctor or an unexpected phone call. They've had to overcome shock, face inconvenient truths, confront shame, and risk career damage. The tsunami of the triggering event compounded by consequent emotions spins them in a vicious cycle and then spits them out to a place of clarity, where they must make choices and communicate with colleagues.

In-depth interviews with several clients, the challenges revealed by others during coaching conversations, and my own experiences with adversity persuade me that every individual's situation and their response to it is unique. All together, these stories point to four effective tactics we can employ to juggle work, a crisis, our families, and ourselves.

Manage the Flow of Information

One of the first decisions involves how to communicate our circumstances to coworkers and how much to disclose. If the issue is in the open, such as a family death that is covered in the news, or visible, as when an individual goes through aggressive cancer treatment, we want to be the first to notify people at work. Initially we may be tempted to shroud seemingly shameful or simply private issues in secrecy, but these challenges are common to the human condition and empathetic colleagues can be a tremendous support. Being the first to provide information also helps us ensure its accuracy.

Some individuals want to openly discuss issues such as mental illness to help bust the stigma that accompanies these widespread struggles. However, when one of our loved ones is suffering, we must also consider their privacy. What's more, revealing a child's condition might make colleagues think we're going to be less reliable, distracted from work, and unable to put in the hours. We also want to be mindful that sharing an ongoing issue is different from revealing our past. Raw and evolving emotions can elicit awkwardness from others who may resort to giving us unsolicited special treatment. Some confidences are best shared only with our closest coworkers, those who will notice changes in our performance and may need to understand and provide accommodations. Managers have additional considerations. As Rhonda said, "I think there can be a danger of oversharing, especially as a boss." Less specificity, such as, "Thank you for asking; I'll share more later," can work for others.

Follow similar guidelines at home when you decide what to disclose. Communicating with children merits special consideration. Aside from obvious factors such as your children's ages, first discuss choices with your partner and start with values you both embrace. We learned of my husband's brother's death after our kids were asleep. We agreed to wait until morning when I would share the news with them. We wanted to be transparent with our children about what happened and to give them space to mourn their loss. Because I delivered the news, they didn't feel pressure to console their dad before processing their own emotions.

Clarify Your Preferences and Expectations

When disclosing our challenges, we want to be clear about what we do or don't want from people. For example, "I'm overwhelmed and unable to process advice or offers for help; the best thing you can do for me is simply listen." Nonnegotiables need to be clear to everyone, such as the daycare pickup time when you have custody of your kids. We determine what medium to use for communication. When Natalya faced the death of a loved one by suicide, she told only two people at work directly, followed by an email to her group. In the email she asked that others continue to treat her as previously because it was too painful for her to discuss the situation.

Many have told me that working helped during a serious challenge if they could set boundaries to address immediate needs and their emotional well-being. According to Rhonda, "Work was an opportunity to control things when lots was going on that I couldn't control.

Work had an accomplishable side to it." If you need time off from work, whether to care for someone else or for your own health, make a clear request, and you will often get what you ask for. "Nobody ever questioned when I needed time to be with my family, which was my biggest ask," Natalya shared.

Take Care of Yourself Every Day

Absolutely nonnegotiable during a crisis is allowing time for daily self-care. We might compromise on the duration but never the occurrence of our rituals. Time spent could be reduced to as little as 10 minutes if necessary or, if we're confronted with a situation likely to trigger more trauma, extra time might be needed. Derek shared, "When I go to big events where it's part of my job to entertain, self-care is even more important. I run each morning and block off an hour each afternoon when I sit and reflect so I can go back refreshed." Self-care encompasses many pursuits: meditation, journaling, playing the guitar, physical exercise, and so forth. Natalya said, "Create space to have mental breathing room so that you can see yourself in what you are doing, and how you are doing it." Another client, who became a dumbbell devotee after his cancer treatments, said, "You have to get physically strong to be work strong."

Self-care helps us get to know ourselves better. Through it, we come to recognize triggers and signs of regression and that changing what's inside our heads has transformational power. Most of my interviewees also advocate professional therapy for themselves and their children, and they also speak of it openly to bust the taboo around it. In fact, the insights offered here aren't substitutes for the support of a mental health practitioner, which I am not. Please consult with one if your challenge merits professional attention. Teletherapy has made this more convenient than ever, even for the busiest among us.

Find Strength in Numbers

Individuals who shared their stories with me all said they wouldn't have transcended their trials alone. Couples often divvied up the load according to their strengths. "I was doing a lot of emotional labor, and my husband was doing the physical labor," said Rhonda. When frequent global traveler Anique's daughter was diagnosed with acute anxiety, she and her husband Eric scheduled 10-year-old Jasmine's therapy appointments on Fridays so they could all attend. On weeks Anique was home, she tackled the heavy lifting at work in the early mornings so she could dedicate dinnertime onward to Jasmine for bedtime rituals. Eric would stay up later to clean up around the kitchen. After three months, they decided to homeschool Jasmine, and Eric took a leave from work to teach her.

Managers leaned more heavily on their teams, leading to both sides benefiting. As one client who took on an expanded role at home said, "Continuity for the kids was a guiding principle. My staff is a lot more capable than they used to be. I'm sure me stepping out created a vacuum, and others stepped into it. I've even been promoted."

Some people rely on a small circle of long-trusted friends. This coven of confidants accepts us, frees us from the need to hide, and helps hold us accountable. One client who simultaneously dealt with divorce, single parenting, and addiction treatment said, "They were either going to accept or reject me, and I was willing to have it be all of me, not just a part of me."

What lies on the other side of a family crisis? Some hardships pass, some become part of our new normal, and many bring us to a better place than before. By confronting the realities of life up close, my clients who have overcome these hardships have learned to make life their priority—to focus on things that really matter whether at work or in their personal lives, starting with themselves. Most say this is the healthiest they've been, others have been promoted at work, and several believe their relationships are stronger than ever. According to Derek, "I'm double my prior self and I'm working less."

From divorces to deaths to drinking and other disruptions, survivors are armed with the confidence derived from overcoming challenges. Another client says, "I realize that all the real changes are inside my own head, and that through love—deep love—those changes occur and are translated into actions of empathy, connection, patience, sharing, and helping that are contagious." Once they're no longer in the clutches of these challenges, they pay it forward; through small acts of kindness, mentorship, and sponsorship, or simply showing up to listen, without judgment. "The more we recognize that the people we're working with all have to deal with these things from time to time," Rhonda shared, "the more compassionate it makes us, the more humane the workplace becomes."

Adapted from "Working Through a Personal Crisis," on hbr.org, July 6, 2020 (product #H05OOJ).

Epilogue

You've Got This

22

Parenting Is Making You a Better Leader

by Peter Bregman

Quick Takes

The skills you use as a parent are the same skills that can make you a great leader. As a parent you've learned to:

- Express care
- Practice patience
- Cultivate independence
- Develop unique strengths
- Set expectations and boundaries
- Pivot and deal with the unexpected

A few days ago I was running in Central Park as fast as I could, pushing myself hard, trying to beat my previous best time.

About halfway around the park I passed a mother walking with her 2-year-old daughter. They were holding hands, and she was moving at the pace of her child, about one step every five seconds.

We were both enjoying ourselves, both in the moment, both focused on our task. But the contrast between us struck me.

I was the equivalent of an individual contributor in an organization. A specialist, striving to maximize my personal productivity and achievement. Specialist jobs are critical to the success of any organization, at all levels of the hierarchy.

She, on the other hand, was the equivalent of a leader, a different and equally critical job in an organization.

Here's what occurred to me: If you're a parent, you're already a leader. And the skills you develop by necessity to be a good parent are precisely the skills you will draw from to be an exceptional leader. It's the same job. Think about it:

Expressing Care

Parents love and care deeply for their children and, from that love, often make sacrifices to do what's best for them.

Great leaders don't simply care about their employee's productivity, they care about their employees. And out of that care; they help employees make the right choices for them, even if these are not in the leader's best interest. I remember one leader, early in my career, for whom I worked as hard as I could. I was his right-hand person. I felt so cared for by him—and trusted him so completely—that when I received a job offer from another organization, I asked him what he thought I should do. We discussed it, and, ultimately, he advised me to take the job because it was in my best interest. We're still friends more than a decade later, and I would still do anything he asked.

Practicing Patience

Let's face it, parenting can sometimes be excruciatingly boring. Successful parents require a tremendous amount of patience.

Likewise, great leaders pace themselves to the unique needs and abilities of each of their employees. They need tremendous patience because it's not about their individual success; it's about the contribution of their teams and the individuals on their teams. Great leaders are motivated by the success of others and recognize that their employees' success is their success. Just like a parent.

The skills you develop by necessity to be a good parent are precisely the skills you will draw from to be an exceptional leader. Great parents don't try to fit their kids into a box. They watch them carefully for signs of natural motivation and inclination and then try to provide opportunities for them to develop further into their areas of interest and passion.

Great leaders know that the best thing they can do for their employees—as well as their companies—is get the right people into the right jobs. Jobs that leverage their unique strengths and mitigate the negative consequences of their weaknesses.

This means that great leaders are always watching, taking note of their employees' personalities, and putting them in the environments where they will be most successful. I know a guy, we'll call him John, who was failing at his job. John loved being with people, but he was a technologist and spent his days coding in a cubicle all day with very little contact with people. The leader of his business noticed this and changed John's role, putting him on a project team. Once John was collaborating with others, his performance shot up.

Developing Independent Capability

Great parents know they have only a few critical years to impact their children, and then, sooner than they imagine, their children will be out of the house. So great parents strive to foster independently capable children. Then, when their peers have more influence over them than their parents, they will still make the right choices.

Likewise, the best leaders build independently capable teams. They coach them to think for themselves. Great leaders know their job is to move their employees up and out of their teams into more challenging opportunities in other areas of the company while continuing to act as mentors and advisers. They nudge their employees out of the safety of the nest.

Setting Appropriate Expectations and Boundaries

If children are unclear about what's acceptable and what's not, they'll freeze, unsure and insecure about whether they can act. The best parents set clear boundaries so their children feel secure and confident. And the best parents set appropriately high expectations so their children know to reach far, allowing for failure without giving up.

The best leaders also have appropriately high expectations of their employees and set clear boundaries about what's acceptable and what's not. And their employees know it and work tremendously hard to live up to those expectations.

Pivoting and Dealing with the Unexpected

When I submitted this article to my editor (also a parent), she reminded me of another reason becoming a great parent leads to becoming a great leader: Children are constantly throwing us curveballs—sometimes on purpose, sometimes because that's life—and as parents, we must develop the resilience to face our own changing and disappointed expectations.

"I can remember at least two big times," she wrote to me, "when I had to bring really bad news to two different parent-bosses—news that would justifiably make them upset—and they basically just shrugged their shoulders and moved forward. They listened and then pivoted to problem solving and exploring scenarios and outcomes. It was such a gift to experience this, as an employee and as a parent."

• • •

Leadership is a learned skill. So is parenting. When you work hard to become a better parent—by reading books, going to classes, experimenting, learning from mistakes—you are also, simultaneously, learning to become a better leader.

Of course, there are differences. The pressure for performance outcomes with a particular employee is often more immediate than with a child. And the relationship is shorter lived: How many of us expect to have the same employees for the next 50 years? Also, if it's not working out, you could fire an employee, but it's unlikely you'd fire your child.

Still, since so many of us spend so much of our time either parenting or working—and these days we're often parenting *and* working at the same time in the same spaces—it's useful to remember that your parenting is not *distracting* you *from* your work, it's *developing* you *for* it.

And conversely, while your work may, at times, be taking you away from your children, it's also helping you show up more fully, more competently, more helpfully, for them.

All this is to say that next time you're in the park, walking at the pace of your 2-year-old, or you're on a road trip with your teen touring colleges, and your boss or a client calls and asks what you're doing, don't hesitate to answer: "leadership development."

Adapted from "Why Parents Make Great Managers," on hbr.org, November 10, 2009 (product #H00405).

NOTES

Chapter 4

1. Gemma Francis, "Parents Have More Than 2,000 Rows with Their Kids Every Year—and They Only 'Win' Half," *Mirror*, July 26, 2018, https://www.mirror.co.uk/lifestyle/health/parents-more-2000-rows-kids-12983598.

Chapter 10

1. Francis J. Flynn and Vanessa K. B. Lake, "If You Need Help, Just Ask: Underestimating Compliance with Direct Requests for Help," *Journal of Personality and Social Psychology* 95, no. 1 (2008): 128–143.

2. Daniel Newark, Francis J. Flynn, and Vanessa K. Bohns, "Once Bitten, Twice Shy: The Effect of a Past Refusal on Future Compliance," *Social Psychology and Personality Science* 5, no. 2 (2014): 218–225.

3. Lara B. Aknin et al., "Making a Difference Matters: Impact Unlocks the Emotional Benefits of Prosocial Spending," *Journal of Economic Behavior and Organization* 88 (2013): 90–95.

Chapter 13

1. Center on Addiction, "The Importance of Family Dinners," September 2012, https://drugfree.org/reports/the-importance-of-family-dinners-viii/.

Chapter 15

1. Dana Goldstein, "Don't Help Your Kids with Their Homework," *Atlantic*, April 2014, https://www.theatlantic.com/magazine/archive/2014/04/and-dont-help-your-kids-with-their-homework/358636/.

ABOUT THE CONTRIBUTORS

DAISY DOWLING, SERIES EDITOR, is the founder and CEO of Workparent, the executive coaching and training firm, and the author of *Workparent: The Complete Guide to Succeeding on the Job, Staying True to Yourself, and Raising Happy Kids* (Harvard Business Review Press, 2021). She is a full-time working parent to two young children. She can be reached at www.workparent.com.

ALISON BEARD is a senior editor at *Harvard Business Review*, cohost of the *Dear HBR:* and *HBR IdeaCast* podcasts, and a grateful mom to two fabulous children, Jack and Ella, and a funny cat, Pickle, who are the lights of her life.

PETER BREGMAN, CEO of Bregman Partners, is recognized as the number-one executive coach in the world by Leading Global Coaches. Author and contributor to 18 books, his most recent book is *Leading with Emotional Courage: How to Have Hard Conversations, Create Accountability, and Inspire Action on Your Most Important Work*. He is also the host of the *Bregman Leadership Podcast*. But his most important roles—and the ones that push him to learn the most—are as husband and father of three kids, all of who see right through him!

SARAH GREEN CARMICHAEL is a former executive editor at *Harvard Business Review.* Follow her on Twitter @skgreen.

TIFFANY DUFU is founder and CEO of The Cru, a peer-coaching network that matches circles of women who collaborate to meet their personal and professional goals. She's also the author of the bestselling book *Drop the Ball: Achieving More by Doing Less.* She's the mother of two tweens who are currently being parented by Fortnite and YouTube in true #droptheball fashion.

BRUCE FEILER is the author of seven consecutive *New York Times* bestsellers, including *Council of Dads: My Daughters, My Illness, and the Men Who Could Be Me*, which inspired the NBC television series, and *The Secrets of Happy Families: Improve Your Mornings, Tell Your Family History, Fight Smarter, Go Out and Play, and Much More.* His latest book is *Life Is in the Transitions: Mastering Change at Any Age.* He lives in Brooklyn with his wife, Linda Rottenberg, and their identical twin daughters, Eden and Tybee.

STEWART D. FRIEDMAN, an organizational psychologist at the Wharton School, is author of three Harvard Business Review Press books—*Total Leadership: Be a Better Leader, Have a Richer Life; Leading the Life You Want: Skills for Integrating Work and Life*; and *Parents Who*

Lead: The Leadership Approach You Need to Parent with Purpose, Fuel Your Career, and Create a Richer Life. He founded the Wharton Leadership Program, the Wharton Work/Life Integration Project, and Total Leadership, a management consulting and training company. His three grown children work in education. He hopes his two grandchildren will help us all heal our broken world.

AMY GALLO is a contributing editor at *Harvard Business Review* and the author of the *HBR Guide to Dealing with Conflict at Work* (Harvard Business Review Press, 2017). She writes and speaks about workplace dynamics. As the parent of a teenager, she spends a lot of time trying to figure out how to apply her own advice on difficult conversations at home. Follow her on Twitter @amyegallo.

HEIDI GRANT is a social psychologist who researches, writes, and speaks about the science of motivation. She is the director of research and development, EY Americas Learning, and serves as associate director of Columbia's Motivation Science Center. She received her doctorate in social psychology from Columbia University. Her most recent book is *Reinforcements: How to Get People to Help You* (Harvard Review Press, 2018). She is also the author of *Nine Things Successful People Do Differently* (Harvard Business Review Press, 2012) and *No One Understands You and What to Do About It* (Harvard Business Review Press, 2015).

WHITNEY JOHNSON is an executive coach, speaker, and innovation thinker recently named one of the most influential management thinkers by Thinkers50. She is the author of *Build an A-Team: Play to Their Strengths and Lead Them Up the Learning Curve* from Harvard Business Press and the critically acclaimed *Disrupt Yourself: Master Relentless Change and Speed Up Your Learning Curve*. She is the wife of one, and mother of two wonderful truth tellers (aka college-age children).

MARY (MOLLY) C. KERN is an organizational psychologist and associate professor of management at Baruch College at the City University of New York. Her research and teaching focus on negotiation processes and team dynamics aimed toward maximizing performance and bounded ethicality to support ethical learners. Although a negotiation scholar, she gets a lot of real-world practice translating the science into more of an art with her two teenagers.

REBECCA KNIGHT is a freelance journalist in Boston whose work has been published in the *New York Times*, *USA Today*, and the *Financial Times*. She is the mom of two tween daughters.

TERRI R. KURTZBERG is an associate professor of management at Rutgers Business School. She is the author of four books, and her research on e-communication and negotiations is frequently quoted in the media. She is the recipient of multiple teaching and research awards. She was especially grateful for her PhD in negotiations when she started raising two kids who were born negotiators, although on any given day it's anyone's guess who has the edge!

SABINA NAWAZ is a global CEO coach, leadership keynote speaker, and writer working in over 26 countries. She advises C-level executives in *Fortune* 500 corporations, government agencies, nonprofits, and academic organizations. Sabina has spoken at hundreds of seminars, events, and conferences, including TEDx, and has written for FastCompany.com, Inc.com, and Forbes.com. She is lucky to have the support of her stay-at-home husband. She counts as successful any meeting that's free of interruption by her two teenage sons or two dogs. A successful day is one spent with them. Follow her on Twitter @sabinanawaz.

CURT NICKISCH is a senior editor at *Harvard Business Review* where he makes podcasts and cohosts *HBR Idea-Cast*. He earned an MBA from Boston University and previously reported for NPR, *Marketplace*, WBUR, and *Fast Company*. He speaks *ausgezeichnet* German and binges history podcasts. Find him on Twitter @CurtNickisch.

ELIZABETH GRACE SAUNDERS is a time management coach and the founder of Real Life E Time Coaching &

Speaking. She is author of *How to Invest Your Time Like Money* and *Divine Time Management: The Joy of Trusting God's Loving Plans for You*. Find out more at www.Real LifeE.com.

AMY JEN SU is a cofounder and managing partner of Paravis Partners, a premier executive coaching and leadership development firm. For the past two decades, she has coached CEOs, executives, and rising stars in organizations. She is the author of the Harvard Business Review Press book *The Leader You Want to Be: Five Essential Principles for Bringing Out Your Best Self—Every Day* and coauthor of *Own the Room: Discover Your Signature Voice to Master Your Leadership Presence* with Muriel Maignan Wilkins. Amy is also a full-time working parent with a teenage son who is currently in high school.

NICOLE TORRES is a former senior editor at *Harvard Business Review.*

ALYSSA F. WESTRING is the Vincent de Paul Associate Professor of Management and Entrepreneurship at DePaul University's Driehaus College of Business. She is the coauthor of *Parents Who Lead: The Leadership Approach You Need to Parent with Purpose, Fuel Your Career, and Create a Richer Life* (Harvard Business Review Press, 2020). She is an award-winning educator and the director of research at Total Leadership. She has two school-age children and lives in Chicago.

INDEX

advice, from other parents,
    41–42
agile development, 11, 117
agile family meetings, 9–16
alternative work arrangements,
    145–150
apps, 103

backup plan, for a sick child,
    153, 154
Bailyn, Lotte, 146, 148
balance
    letting go of idea of, 55–64
    See also work-life balance
Beard, Alison, 35–43
boss
    explaining time away from
        work to, 129
    gaining support for flexible
        work from, 145–150
    oversharing with, 174
    selling remote work to,
        104
boundaries, setting, 119,
    124–125, 141, 175–176,
    187–188
brain research, 14
Bregman, Peter, 183–189
Broken Compass study, 130

calendars
    blocking out time on, 160
    color-coding, 72
    electronic, 19
    look-aheads, 73
    operationalizing, 71–72
    pre-blocks, 72
    syncing family, 17–23
care, expressing, 184
Carmichael, Sarah Green,
    76–81
change, getting comfortable
    with, 62
charismatic leaders, 15
childcare, 21, 119, 154
children
    active dialogue with, 72–74
    checkpoints with, 70
    Covid-19 pandemic and,
        115–126
    demands of older, 66–67
    education of, 128
    empowering, 14
    explaining remote work
        arrangement to, 104
    family crisis and, 171–179
    family meals and, 107–114
    helping grown, 126
    independent, 133, 187
    interactions with, 59–60

children (*continued*)
negotiating with your, 25–33
offering choices to, 31
quality time with, 63
school-age, demands of, 127–133
setting boundaries for, 124
sick, 151–157
working from home with, 99–105
choices, offering to kids, 31
chores, 117, 121–122
chronic illness, 156–157
Clifton Strengths Finder, 5–6
colleagues
communication with, 156, 173–174
engaging with, 37–38
explaining time away from work to, 129
flexible work arrangements and, 148–149
oversharing with, 174
relationship building with, 103
remote work and, 102
saying no to requests from, 89–95
communication
about family crisis, 173–175
about a sick child, 153
with children, 72–74
with colleagues, 156, 173–174
with family members, about work, 166–169
with partner, 120

contributions, parenting, 67–71
conversations. *See* communication
Covid-19 pandemic, xv
getting things done during, 115–126
taking long view of, 126
teaching opportunities during, 118

D3 reviews, 117
delegation, 75–81
imaginary, 78
time conflicts and, 162
Dillon, Karen, 91–95
dinnertime, 107–114, 121
Dowling, Daisy, xiii–xvii, 99–105, 107–114, 127–133, 151–157
Dufu, Tiffany, 75–81

EdNavigator, 130
electronic calendars, 19
emergency fund, 155
emergency meals, 113
emotions, in family negotiations, 27
entitlement, 7
executive skills, 14
expectations
adjusting your, 94, 137
clarifying your, 175–176
of others, 169

setting, 141, 187–188
unrealistic, 77, 136
extended families, 37

Facebook, 156
fairness, 32
families
culture of, 161
extended, 37
rituals for, 50
See also family members
family calendars
color-coding, 72
look-aheads, 73
operationalizing, 71–72
pre-blocks, 72
syncing, 17–23
family crisis, 171–179
family goals, 60–61
family meals, 107–114, 121
family meetings
agile, 9–16
weekly, 20–21
family members
contributions to dinner by,
112–113
conversations with, 64,
72–74, 166–169
discussing priorities with, 50
identifying and developing
strengths of, 5–6
input from, 5
negotiating with, 25–33
treating as important, 6
See also children; spouse

family study hall, 131
fathers. *See* parents
feedback, negative, 94
Feiler, Bruce, 9–16
flexibility, 15–16, 101–102
flexible work arrangements
gaining support for, 145–150
organizational benefits of,
149
reassessing and adjusting,
149–150
team input on, 148–149
trial period for, 147–148
See also remote work;
working from home
focus, 63, 140
Friedman, Stewart D., 55–64,
148–150, 165–169
friends
help from, 35–43
support from, during crisis,
178

Galinsky, Ellen, 10
Gallo, Amy, 145–150
goals
alignment of work and
family, 60–61
for flexible work
arrangements, 147
See also priorities
grandparents
helping grown kids, 126
as teachers, 118–119
Grant, Adam, 39

Index

Grant, Heidi, 40, 83–88, 136–142
gratitude, 122
growth mindset, 138
guilt
    over time conflicts, 160
    over to-do list, 135–142

habits, 62, 71
harmony, 59
help
    asking for, 40–41, 83–88
    offering your, 39–40
    saying no to requests for, 89–95
    saying thank you for, 88
home life
    happier, 3–7, 10
    keeping sane, 165–169
    scheduling, 4–5
    See also work-life balance
homeschooling, 118–119
homework, 131

imaginary delegation, 78
independence, 133, 187
information flows
    about family crisis, 173–175
    See also communication

job constraints, 161
Johnson, Whitney, 3–7, 137–141

Kanban boards, 117
Kern, Mary C., 25–33
kids. See children
Knight, Rebecca, 89–95, 135–142
Kurtzberg, Terri R., 25–33

late-night work, 122
leadership, 15, 56, 60, 62, 183–189
lifelines, offering, 93
limitations, recognizing your, 138–139
lockdown, getting things done during, 115–126
long-term thinking, 51–52
look-aheads, 73

meal time, 107–114, 121
micromanagement, 59–60
mindset, 58, 59, 109, 138
mothers. See parents

nap time, 120
Nawaz, Sabina, 171–179
negative feedback, 94
negative ruminations, 137
negotiations, with kids, 25–33
networks, building, 35–43
Nickisch, Curt, 56–64
"no," learning to say, 89–95

offers, in negotiations, 31
outsourcing, 119

parenting
    personal nature of, 48
    skills from, 183–189
    as source of power, 56–57
    spending time wisely,
        65–74
parenting posse, 35–43
parents
    asking for help from other,
        40–41
    defining contributions and
        passions as, 67–71
    engaging with other, 37–38
    invincibility of, 15
    learning from other, 41–42
    micromanagement by,
        59–60
    offering help to, 39–40
    patience required by, 185–
        186
    support from other, 35–43
    See also working parents
parent-teacher relationship,
    131–132
partner
    making time to connect
        with, 120
    support from, 177–178
passions, parenting, 67–71
patience, 185–186
pediatricians, 155

personal commitments, com-
    peting with professional
    commitments, 159–163
personal crisis, managing work
    during, 171–179
phone calls
    privacy during, 102
    responding to, 81
    when working from home,
        102
pivoting, 188
planning time, 63–64
positive self-talk, 142
power struggles, with kids,
    28–29
present, being, 63
priorities
    communicating with your
        partner about, 120
    defining importance of,
        51–52
    discussing with family, 50
    family meals as, 109–110
    fusing with schedule, 52–53
    parenting, 67–71
    setting, 49–50, 77, 140,
        160–161
    values-driven schedule and,
        47–53
productivity, 101–102, 138
professional commitments,
    competing with personal
    commitments, 159–163
project management software,
    64

questions, asking kids,
    29–30

reciprocity, 39–40
reference points, 32
reframing situations, 137
relationship building, 37–38,
    103
remote work
    benefits of, 100
    challenges of, 100
    connecting family with, 121
    demonstrating commitment
        and, 102
    explaining to kids, 104
    going to office and, 103–104
    keeping routine and,
        101–102
    with kids, 99–105
    making case for, 101
    physical work environment
        for, 102–103
    relationship building and,
        103
    selling to boss, 104
    technology for, 103
    See also working from home
repetition, in family
    negotiations, 27
requests
    assessing, 91–92
    saying no to, 89–95
resilience, 188
rituals, family, 50
Rozman, Ariela, 130

Saunders, Elizabeth Grace,
    17–23, 47–53, 159–163
schedule
    family calendars for, 17–23
    for home life, 4–5
    values-driven, 47–53
    See also calendars; time
        management
school-age kids, 127–133
school volunteerism, 129–130
screen time, 63, 122
self-care, 176–177
self-empathy, 142
sick child, 151–157
silence, in negotiations, 32–33
Slack, 103
snacks, 112
social media, 156
space, respecting others, 121
spouse
    making time to connect
        with, 120
    support from, 177–178
"sprint and recover" approach,
    131
stakeholder dialogues, 166–169
strengths, identifying and
    developing, 5–6
stress, 10, 128
Su, Amy Jen, 65–74
support networks
    during Covid-19 pandemic,
        125
    during crises, 177–178
    of other parents, 35–43
Sutherland, Jeff, 12

take out, 112
tasks
   asking for help with, 83–88
   delegating, 75–81
   on to-do lists, 139–141
   outsourcing, 119
   turning down extra, 89–95
teachers, 131–132
technology audit, 103
thank yous, 88
time commitments, competing,
   159–163
time management
   conflicting commitments
     and, 159–163
   delegation and, 76–81
   with family calendars,
     17–23
   family meals and, 111
   for homework, 131
   values-driven schedule and,
     47–53
   working parents and, 48–49,
     65–74
to-do lists
   being pragmatic about,
     139–140
   guilt over, 135–142
   paring down, 117, 139–140
Torres, Nicole, 77–81
trade-offs, 59
Twitter, 156

unexpected, dealing with the,
   188

values
   reflecting on your, 58
   time commitments and,
     161–162
   transmitting, 61–62
values-driven schedule, 47–53
video calls, 102–103
virtual presence, 162–163
vision, 60
volunteer commitments,
   129–130

waterfall model of software
   development, 12
Weeks, Holly, 91–95
Westring, Alyssa, 55–64
win-win agreements, 28
work
   commitments at, conflicting
     with personal, 159–163
   dedicated time for, 122–123
   during family crisis, 171–179
   flexible arrangements,
     145–150
   increased commitments at,
     165–169
   late-night, 122
   sick child and, 151–157
   stepping back from,
     123–124
work ethic, 102
work goals, 60–61
working from home
   benefits of, 100
   challenges of, 100

working from home
(*continued*)
demonstrating commitment
when, 102
explaining to kids, 104
going to office and, 103–104
keeping routine while,
101–102
with kids, 99–105
making case for, 101
physical work environment
for, 102–103
relationship building and,
103
selling to boss, 104
staggering your day and, 116
technology for, 103
See also remote work
working parents
Covid-19 pandemic and,
115–126
demands of school-age kids
and, 127–133

expectations for, 48, 66
family meals and, 107–114
flexible work arrangements
for, 145–150
learning from other, 41–42
overwhelmed, xiii–xv, 58
pressures on, 10, 66
reflection by, 58–59
sick child and, 151–157
staggering of day by, 116
support from other parents
for, 35–43
time management and,
48–49, 65–74
volunteer commitments and,
129–130
See also parents
work-life balance
keeping sane, 165–169
letting go of idea of, 55–64
spending time wisely for,
65–74